The Evolution
of Belief

J. Gregory Steiner

The Evolution of Belief

A Christian Perspective for the Future

ARCHWAY
PUBLISHING

Archway Publishing books may be ordered through booksellers or by contacting:

Archway Publishing
1663 Liberty Drive
Bloomington, IN 47403
www.archwaypublishing.com
1 (888) 242-5904

ISBN: 978-1-4808-6384-2 (sc)
ISBN: 978-1-4808-6383-5 (hc)
ISBN: 978-1-4808-6385-9 (e)

Library of Congress Control Number: 2018907262

The Jerusalem Bible © 1966 by Darton Longman &
Todd Ltd and Doubleday and Company Ltd.

Print information available on the last page.

Archway Publishing rev. date: 6/26/2018

Contents

Acknowledgments ix

Introduction xi

1. The Truth in Stories 1
2. The God Experience in Our Lives 9
3. Changing Some Traditional Starting Points 16
   God as an Unverifiable Focus for an Act of Faith 17
   Matter Has a Radical Capacity for Life 20
   The Emergence of *Homo Sapiens* 23
4. Revisiting Some Treasured Religious Concepts 27
   Creation 28
   The Incarnation 31
   The Redemption 39
   The Adam and Eve Myth Goes Viral 41
   What It Means to Be Free 43
5. Textual Criticism, an Inside Look 46
   Example 1: Early Manuscript Writing and Context 49
   Example 2: St. Luke and the Humanity of Jesus 50
   Example 3: St. Paul and Women in the Church 52
   Two Resolutions 54
6. Conscience Formation in Modern Times 57
   The Nature of Conscience 58
   Origin of Moral Laws 58
   Challenges that Science and Technology
   Bring to Decision-Making 61
   In Vitro Fertilization 61
   Vaccination 64

7. The Power of Good and Evil................................ 67
    Ancient Spirits 68
    Blaming a Deity: the Easy Way Out...................... 69
    The Devil Did Not Make Me Do It 71
    Exorcism 72
    Free Will or Not.......................................74
    Relating Free Will to Religious Precepts 76
8. Science, a Potential Ally for Purifying Christian Belief.... 78
    Decision-Making and the Informed Conscience 78
    Family Planning....................................... 81
    Contraception... 83
    Abortion.. 84
    Assisted Death 86
    Masturbation.. 89
    Premarital Sex 91
    The Paranormal.. 95
    Homosexuality and Related Issues...................... 97
9. Ceremony and Ritual: Outward Expressions of Faith 103
    Celebrations Are for Everyone 105
    Christmas Is a Universal Favorite..................... 106
    Easter as the Final Act of Surrender 108
    Sacraments and Sacramentals 109
    The Sacraments of Initiation 110
    The Magician and the Magic 111
    Sacraments of Healing 115
    Reconciliation 116
    Anointing of the Sick.................................117
    Sacraments of Vocation 118
    Matrimony 119
    Holy Orders 121
10. Dualism: Can the Soul Survive? 125
    What Is Soul?... 126
    Ancient Understanding of the Soul.................... 128
    The Body of Evidence 129

Immateriality 129
The Frustration of Science with the
Theology of the Soul 132
The Human Dynamo: the New Shift 134
Implications for a Religious Point of View 135
Will the Human Dynamo Persist Indefinitely? 136
11. Life-after-Death Issues, Where Analogy Abounds 138
Faith in Life after Death 139
A Visionary with a Futuristic Analogy 140
Use of Analogy in Science 142
Analogy Applied to *Homo Sapiens* and Darwinism 143
New Beginnings Applied to a Personal Life after Death 144
Beginnings, Not Endings 146
Conclusion 150
12. The Certainty of Faith and Science 152
The Certainty of Faith 154
The Certainty of Fact 157
The Final Word 160

Endnotes 163
Bibliography 173

Acknowledgments

I would like to express my deepest gratitude to my wife, Carol, and my son, Michael, for their insights into science and theology. Without their support and encouragement, this book would not have been written.

Introduction

Have you ever observed the disintegration of grocery bags? Over a period of just a few months, I witnessed the gradual and near-total dissolution of a grocery bag stuck between the sharp points of two branches on a tree. After a short amount of time, the bag lost its color, thinned out, and gradually shrank, collapsing into many pieces, carried away by the wind. On the other hand, if I were to go down to my storage room, I would come upon a large array of bags with packed items that, over a period of time, seem to grow, much the way certain crystals grow in a bottle. Frustrating as it is, the problem of excess baggage does not disappear in the sun and wind and rain, as grocery bags do. As we continually collect boxes and suitcases, we have to judge what might be relevant and important to us in the future. It is true that baggage, unlike grocery bags, could last for thousands of years beyond our lifetimes, as long as there is someone who finds the contents interesting, valuable, and worth keeping.

In much the same way, a host of accumulated familial, social, cultural, and religious items sits in our neural pathways, stored with the hope, conviction, and belief that they might be important to us at some point in time. This type of baggage could possibly be beneficial in that it brings back memories and allows us to accept and celebrate our past community experiences. Finally, a baggage of memories does tell us many things. It is much like Tevye in *Fiddler on the Roof* as he sings out in boisterous defense to his daughters that the Jewish tradition is important because it tells us who we are and where we have been. Admittedly, how would one know where one is going without knowing where one has been? To Tevye, tradition was very important, but to his somewhat liberated daughters, some traditions appeared not to be that important.

From the outset, the reader should know that my book is not pastoral in nature or purpose and that it greatly favors a critical and scientific point of view regarding Christian belief. In addition, I do not specify what is to happen in religious studies classes or the thoughts behind a homily at a church service.

My book targets educated Christians—that is, men and women who have been at least somewhat versed in the sciences and understand evolution and its evidence in nature. I suggest that the inquirer be well aware that the new religious insights proposed here could be shocking, especially when I find the need to erect new concepts of belief based on a new paradigm or worldview. With regard to humanity's discovery of God, I suggest that "risen primates," rather than "fallen angels,"[1] be the accepted and more credible stance when explaining human nature. The term *risen* is not like the traditional understanding of resurrection, and the term *fallen* loses all relevance to this work.

Although I possess some insights from an education in secular society, important and rich religious traditions persist in my mind. This is good. However, there are some obvious and troubling contradictions on the horizon. Religious beliefs are important, and yet they can generate disconcerting feelings, arising whenever the church (Catholic or Protestant) insists on a total and mandatory acceptance of ancient doctrines and dogmatic statements. This work hopes to clarify why some beliefs are relevant and some are in need of replacement if we want to enrich our Christian faith in today's world of science.

In addition, I show how important religious and cultural traditions are for a better understanding of what faith is really about. Such traditions, taken together and packed in the suitcases of our minds, tell us a great deal. In our Christian experience, it is very difficult to separate out some aspects of cultural traditions from religious traditions because over centuries the two have been solidly welded together to form this baggage we call Christian belief. It is not the scope of this work to separate out such things, only to know that religious and cultural traditions are not the same. A sharp eye and mind can discern these differences as they appear in the New Testament. Our spiritual lives revolve around a core of what I call baggage, some of which I am embarrassed to say is useless, and this spiritual and cultural baggage may unfortunately hang around for thousands of years. My intent in this book is to focus on the spiritual baggage and only treat our cultural traditions as they overlap into our belief systems.

Evolution, as treated in this work, means a progression outward around a core. Although my history and past career have been in biology as well as theology, I prefer to apply not a strict biological definition (descent with modification) but a progression out from a center, a progression that is steeped in random insights into what now comprises a contemporary Christian belief. As a guilty and remorseful defendant might feel before a judge in court, I can only say, "It is what it is!" This work will not please everyone, but it is my hope it will enlighten the reader into a deeper appreciation of what I put forward as basic principles of Christian belief.

For the reader, I am approaching tenets and practices of a religious nature as an evolutionary and ever-changing phenomenon. I have pointed out some key changes in belief spanning the years from early Hebrew belief to the years of our modern society. The external pressures for changes in belief are reminiscent of the development of new life-forms in plants and animals. A religious belief either adjusts (adapts) to pressures of competition for change or suffers the consequences of disbelief and lack of credibility.

Although this is not a pastoral work and does not attempt to delve into the richness of prayer life and such spiritual matters, the reader will find some topics relating to liturgical acts discussed and examined. Within each chapter, there are components that will move the believer forward into a new belief experience, but I do not attempt to direct pastors on how to instruct the faithful.

Be aware that I will not concentrate on beliefs coming from a traditional idea of revelation. This work discusses insights supported by verifiable scientific evidence. For example, doctrines and dogmas sourced as revelations from a god or supreme being are not scientifically verifiable items, and I treat these from another way of thinking. In this book, revelations are more like discoveries of God. However, this would be a discovery within a creative process of the mind, rather than in a revealed edict.

The first five chapters show us how we can not only assign value to our faith but enhance this faith as well. We accomplish this through storytelling, sharing an experience of God in community, accommodating traditional thought to what we know in modern times, and revisiting essential mysteries of faith and the way we understand the changes occurring in biblical translations. Chapters 6, 7, and 8 treat the nature of conscience, our response to the problem of good and evil, and the support science provides for understanding and resolving contemporary moral issues. Ceremony and ritual are treated in chapter 9, which focuses on the evolution of Christian celebrations and the sacraments of the church. Chapters 10 and 11 propose a different philosophical understanding of soul and life-after-death issues. Chapter 12 concludes with an examination of the certainty of faith, as opposed to the certainty of science.

An additional reminder for the reader is the need to distinguish between belief and faith. Simply put, belief is a conviction arising from a religious community and given to us for enhancing our faith. Faith is a virtuous act of loyalty to a supreme being. I use the metaphor often in my book that faith is a clothesline hung up for all to see. Our beliefs would be the clothes hanging on that faith line. We can alter beliefs over generations or even replace them with new and insightful ones. While beliefs should engender and support a deeper faith over the years, they should never lead us to a static experience that never changes. Faith can never be set in stone. Furthermore, faith assumes a fidelity to something or someone whose existence is not evident from a physical point of view. This situation always includes doubt, found in all levels of religious devotion.

Lastly, our inquiring minds generate wisdom whenever we experience important and integrating events in life. So also a true faith experience will enrich wisdom in our lives when we can minimize certain irrational assumptions of faith and allow other items of belief to become at least somewhat credible. Yes, the intent of this work is not to destroy our lives of faith but rather to enhance our faith in a modern world filled with science and technology. In this instance, I speak of a kind of science that was not available to enhance the lives of early Christian believers. Enjoy the book.

1

The Truth in Stories

I have always believed that stories change over the years. For example, in the sixth grade our class played a sentence game. The teacher whispered into the first student's ear a sentence that by the time it reached my ear did not make much sense. By the time the last student heard the sentence, it was unrecognizable and completely different from the words spoken to the first student. I thought it was just a game, not realizing that the teacher could have been trying to tell us something about the meaning of words and verbal thought transmission. Then again, the teacher may have been trying to show us that we need to speak carefully and clearly when conveying a message.

Another example is my mother, Louise. She died just before her ninety-sixth birthday, and until her last days, she was as sharp as a tack. Prior to her death, my sister and brother-in-law put together, in booklet form, a synopsis of her life in question-and-answer form. They asked her questions like "How do you remember your brothers and sister?" and "What was your favorite pastime as a young girl?" Her responses were very simple yet very personal and truthful. However, when it came to matters that involved her children, Louise had at times a different idea or picture of events from ours. When relating a past story to the six of us, there were times we looked at one another and smiled, occasionally challenging her about the veracity of her memory. She would reply, "Yes, yes, that is exactly how it happened, and don't argue with me about it." The reader may also have good examples of memories of personal experiences altered by transmission and time.

As we remember events, a multistoried version may surface, challenging the veracity of the story. However, the relationship of love and fond memory seems to be more important than the details of the story. When recalling personal experiences within the family, why would one argue about the truth of some petty event or passing opinion? In this chapter, I would like to approach the Christ in Christianity in a similar vein. We all have our experience of Christ through Christian tradition, biblical stories found in the New Testament, sermons and teachings of our church leaders, and endless other sources. Are these experiences true and valid ones? I would be the last one to judge whether the reader has met the real Christ because the real Christ in Christianity is a very personal experience that must always accommodate the place and time in which we live. Furthermore, as we look back over two thousand years, we can see that the understanding of the Christian experience has not been the same for everyone. Christ, as a living person, lives and inspires believers within the context of any given age. This being said, over centuries there exists a continuity of Christian faith that allows us to meet the Christ of our age. As Christians, we believe that Christ is present to us in our faith and He will live forever. However, accompanying these Christ experiences are innumerable traditional beliefs, like baggage carried about for ages, some valuable and some not worth carrying around, like empty grocery bags blowing in the winds of time.

As the well-versed theological exegete will admit, one can always find a reason why an ancient biblical account persists over the decades and centuries. We pass on by word of mouth an event containing traditional memories important to a group of people. A story tells us something. In Hebrew tradition, a story predates any Hebrew script, and these stories are passed on by word of mouth. We can learn something from a good story. I might say, with all due respect to the learned men and women who have spent their lives expounding the history behind a story, that most scholars will focus on the lesson of a moral truth, a sociological truth, or any truth other than a factual and historical placement of that truth. This is not to say one cannot speak about an actual flood at the time of Noah, a figure derived from several ancient traditions. Today, we learn little by reviewing a theory about the location of an ark. We gain much more by investigating why leaders would pass on these stories. Could it be that these writers discovered and then attempted to illustrate humans as capable of doing wrong, actually doing wrong, and needing God in their lives? The Noah figure then becomes important. If people are not habitually good and instead continually do bad things, they will "drown" in their ignorance. I believe this is what the ancient Israelites are saying.

Although the Adam and Eve narrative in the garden of paradise is found in the Torah, it is not solely the claim of Hebrew history. Other ancient traditions claim it as well. The Judeo-Christian tradition relating to Adam's fall finds itself on the pinnacle of importance today because later scholars in Christian times used the myth to expound new lessons surrounding the nature of the first and "original" sin. Unfortunately, we have spilled more ink over the perceived theological implications of the original sin than the very lesson behind this shared story. Regarding the fall of Adam, heated discussions have arisen regarding the translated texts from Greek to Latin by Saint Jerome. In recent times, the nature of original sin has been associated with death (we are all supposed to share in Adam's sin and death). A sin became more important than the lesson to be learned.[2] Many readers of Genesis will note that there were at least four accounts of humanity's fall from grace. These accounts in early Hebrew history were more than likely of equal importance, whether it be the Adam and Eve story, the Cain and Abel episode, the narrative of Noah and his ark floating somewhere off the coast of Turkey, the Tower of Babel, or, last but not the least, the Sodom and Gomorrah tragedy. In the most primitive traditions, these stories all teach the same lesson. People can do wrong, people indeed do wrong, and people need God to fix things.

With a brief look at Old Testament figures and events, the reader discovers the subtleties of truth in a story, the purpose of which is to illustrate a lesson around a traditionally accepted event. These ancient stories lived on by word of mouth long before they were committed to script. Each clan, tribe, and nation altered the story as was fitting for telling it according to specific traditions. Knowing the nature of communication, it would not be logical to expect there to be unanimity of accounts in the story even within a specific population. For example, within our Christian tradition there exist two separate accounts of the creation of humans in the book of Genesis. We should not dismiss stories thought to be only myth, and we should not accept only those accounts thought to be literally true. It is important that we learn a lesson from all our biblical myths and stories. The learned lesson constitutes the truth of the matter as proposed by the person passing on the story. Thus, the story becomes the framework around which we transmit some kind of truth.

Lastly, in our discussion about truth in stories, I ask the reader to avoid thinking that stories told are just stories and have no other value than that of being an entertaining way to learn or pass something on to later generations. These are not just relational events, which are truths only to people at specific times in the past and, as such, have no value in present times. Stories told and lessons learned in ancient history have helped provide the fabric of Western civilization as it is exists today. That is to say, Western civilization's economic, political, and religious structures have developed from a Judeo-Christian background, regardless of our opinion about it. Particular stories in the Old Testament are universally inspirational in nature, in that they invite believers to a higher level of good and honest living. We can say the same about the New Testament writings.

Concerning early Christianity, understanding the truth of a story becomes much more problematic. There are many reasons why there are challenges when searching for kernels of truth among the many accounts of early Christian disciples relating to the presence of Christ and His disciples. While treating a few of these challenges, at no time am I asking the reader to accept some accounts in the New Testament and not to accept the twenty-seven books as a whole. Accept the whole bundle, and move on with those accounts that provide, at this time, a realistic and faith-enhancing potential. Every event and directive in the New Testament has a "truth of the story," which may at times be deeply buried over centuries of storytelling about Jesus and His disciples. Nonetheless, it is still there. Some reasons that challenge the truth of a story are as follows.

Reason 1: The origin of the account is colored by the need to communicate more easily to a specific audience. The author had a specific audience to whom he was proselytizing, whether it was the Jewish community around Jerusalem, the Jewish community spread out around the Mediterranean (the Diaspora), or the Gentiles.

Reason 2: The intent of the writer of each manuscript was perhaps clear only to the writer himself. Each of the gospel writers needed to draw some connection to convince his audience. Matthew explained that Jesus was the fulfillment of all the hopes and aspirations of earlier and ancient Jewish communities and that the kingdom of heaven had arrived. Mark saw Jesus as the mysterious "Son of Man," bearing the secret troves of the kingdom of heaven under the banner of the crucified Messiah. Luke wrote about Jesus as the bearer of loving kindness from the Father, with noticeable references to the Holy Spirit. John, the "beloved disciple," connected Jesus's public life with Jewish celebratory feasts, which found fulfillment in the resurrection. All of these evangelists had a story to tell in their own context.

Reason 3: The gospels had access to an earlier Aramaic text, reworked by Mark,[3] with some episodes either abridged or altered to assist in the missionary activities of the early communities. The meaning and possible accuracy of some parables and "healing episodes" are less clear, or may be lost altogether. However, the figure and position of Christ as savior are still very clear throughout the many centuries to follow.

Reason 4: The letters to early Christian communities carry a mixture of directives (mostly Jewish directives) that do not align themselves clearly with Jesus's directives. There are more than likely some works that did not survive the cuts made by the more institutionally structured Christian religion beginning in the fourth century.[4]

Reason 5: The New Testament manuscripts instruct the reader from the standpoint of a postresurrection experience. From this position, certain religious ceremonies and practices quickly arose within the early Christian community. The community embellished the belief that Jesus not only had risen from the dead but would be returning soon to establish His kingdom. Furthermore, the end of the world was imminent. These convictions could only have altered what lessons Jesus was preaching to fit in line with distinct beliefs of the first disciples.

Reason 6: The idiomatic themes found in Jesus's words are, at times, lost in translation. Even the most astute scholar will admit that portions of the Aramaic phrasing were not understood by all the disciples, let alone understood when translated into Greek. St. Jerome, translating both Greek and some Latin manuscripts into the Vulgate, could only work from the manuscripts before him and what had been passed on in tradition to believers of his time.

There are undoubtedly more reasons that could be discussed. I have chosen these because they will surface in the following chapters as starting points for showing how Christianity follows the typical evolution of any organization. Some contemporary theologians maintain that proclamations of divine inspiration guiding the early disciples did not need to address the context of the times and intent of the New Testament writer because God led the pen to write the absolute truth of what Jesus spoke. However, divine inspiration will never address changes that occur in society, and the status quo is never an option, even in the spiritual mind. In addition, we should remember that the truth behind a story is always more important than the story itself or the various accounts given about a story. Lastly, the value in a story is more than just a lesson to be learned. There is always an additional enrichment to be experienced as we learn more about early Christians and the challenges they encountered.

The science of textual criticism (treated in a later chapter) has had a terrific influence upon the truth of a story. What is important for the reader to understand is the overall purpose of finding value in a biblical story, and not the verifiable or unverifiable intricacies within the story itself.

2

The God Experience in Our Lives

There are pastimes that attract some individuals more than others. I really like doing jigsaw puzzles. Ever since childhood, I have had multiple completed pictures placed here and there, under my bed or as varnished pictures hanging on the wall. Canadian winters can be somewhat confining at times, but for me, putting together puzzles has always been a delightful winter activity. Have you ever tried putting together a puzzle without first seeing the picture? It is truly a challenge. Now, without seeing the picture, take that two-dimensional puzzle and imagine it as a moving, three-dimensional puzzle. The problem is that the piece we are trying to fit is only a static, flat piece with two dimensions. We now have a conundrum or a rather unsolvable dilemma. In a similar way, when trying to explain a God experience and define it for someone else, we are invariably at a loss for words. When we discover God, it is like working on a puzzle we cannot see. We are never satisfied with the incomplete picture of God put together in our minds. In this chapter, I will show how we got to where we are in a God relationship and why we need to move on to a newer look at a God experience.

Throughout all the accounts in Holy Scripture are innumerable instances where men and women have had God experiences.

Associated with all of these personal and spiritual encounters are the hearts of people becoming "enthused"—that is, filled with God. These are the biblical leaders, who stand out in history as being important and great persons. God encounters appeared to be with persons who later changed and altered the course of biblical history. Starting with Adam, through Noah, Abraham, Moses, David, and numerous less notable figures, each one had an encounter that led to a change in the course of biblical history. In the garden of paradise, this encounter was with a deity, personified as a friend, walking alongside our first parents, directing them in matters of what to do and not to do. As such, we cannot understand the story as it is given to us today. After all, how important is the command not to eat of a special fruit? However, what is important is that humans had encountered God as a forceful figure. The believer had to take God seriously. Absolute obedience and worship were necessary if one wanted to achieve a good life and be successful. The same occurs with all the other figures in the Old Testament. Whether it be allusions to an almighty God, powerful beyond all comprehension, an angel of some sort (possibly added on in a much later insertion), or even an ordinary man, as in the book of Tobit, it was always an experience with an all-powerful deity. Beginning with Moses, the chosen people experienced God as the warrior, destroyer of all who abused, imprisoned, killed, and prevented the chosen ones from the reoccupation of a land that was somehow their predestined land of Israel. Mass slaughter of the innocents took place in the name of Israel (God).

In the Old Testament, the Almighty (whose name could not be spoken) was a strict and law-enforcing figure whose presence was important for the nation of Israel to survive. A tribal structure was set up from the outset for erecting a lasting tribute to God the all-powerful. Jerusalem became the center of all Jewish influence as written later by the scribes. In the Bible, Hebrew fidelity was considered paramount. If Israel did as God directed, then the nation would persist. We know that did not happen, and Jerusalem fell to foreigners in the seventh century BCE. These exiled people became the remnants of those who did not follow the commands of God. This is how the scriptural writers defined the failure of such a great nation, but more than likely, the strength of the Assyrian armies had more to do with the first fall of Jerusalem. At any rate, the presence of God was that of an eternal and powerful king, who directed all the events of the chosen people of Israel.

With the advent of Jesus Christ, some radically different experiences of God began to surface. At the time of Jesus, there were some men moving in and out of the Hebrew landscape. These individuals, classified as zealots, not only threatened the status quo with regard to traditional Hebrew tradition but also were also capable of upsetting the relatively peaceful relationship between the Jewish rulers and Rome's overall military control and taxation potential in Palestine. We could easily classify Jesus as a common zealot, i.e., a troublemaker, and He probably was such. Similarities stop at this point. As a zealot, Jesus did not enjoy being an intrusive factor in the daily lives of people. For the most part, His purpose was to bring a novel message, a message of fulfilment, rather than to challenge the law of Moses. Given that elements of His teaching exist in parable forms, we can decipher what He was actually teaching, in spite of the many alterations (redactions) that have taken place as postresurrection indoctrination.

The Holy Spirit in Jesus's teaching was definitely unique and different from that of Judaic tradition in that, far from being the vengeful God, the Holy Spirit was forgiving, fulfilling, strengthening in adversity, breathing life, calming the soul, and lastly, synonymous with peace. Instances in the New Testament that exhibit God's wrath and anger, devastation and death, were more than likely alterations and attributes inserted by later writers who were preaching the "wrath of the Old Testament God," rather than the forgiveness mandate of Jesus.

A glaring example of misunderstanding about the Holy Spirit in the early Christian community occurred in the Acts of the Apostles.[5] Ananias and his wife, Sapphira, withheld from the disciples information about an income source related to a property matter. For some reason, either valid or deceptive, their commitment of money and property to the Christian commune did not cover all that they had, and we are told that they lied about it. As a result, Ananias and Sapphira met their demise by the power of the Holy Spirit. However, upon reading the episode, the more credible explanation is that someone murdered the couple for apparent failure to disclose wealth, or for other reasons. It seems almost certain that the episode is not factual, since there is an attribution to the Holy Spirit of an act contravening the message of peace and forgiveness that resides at the very heart of Jesus's good news. There are other violent episodes involving the Holy Spirit, episodes which we could also question as being truthful or accurate.

We can understand the extent of the early Christians' idea of a vengeful Holy Spirit if we remember that this community lived as if the final coming of Jesus was imminent. They were to witness the "end time" prior to the death of the first disciples. All communes, even in modern times, struggle to exist, oftentimes ending in dissolution or necessarily having to adapt. It is very interesting to note that later accomplishments of Peter and Paul were made possible with the help of converts from Judaism and families from other religious beliefs. These converts were not part of communes, but rather individuals moving about their villages and cities, living a normal lifestyle as workers and tradesmen such as tent making.

In fact, we find St. Paul, the tent maker, residing with a few families on his journeys through the Middle East.

By the time of the fall of Jerusalem (70 CE),[6] the Christian community, as highlighted in Acts of the Apostles, had begun to evolve into something different. Christian monasticism, although not formally appearing until the late second century, more than likely evolved from the type of life that St. John the Evangelist exhibited in some of his letters. Exclusive and secluded communities, such as the ancient Essenes,[7] actually existed in the second century BCE, and they certainly influenced early Christian communities by their strict beliefs in voluntary poverty, celibacy, common property, and personal holiness.

In St. John's gospel and the Book of Revelation, the expansion of the God experience is strikingly evident as he refers to the Spirit as almost an eschatological (end of the world) presence. In his later years, waiting for the final return of the Messiah, John waxes strongly about the Spirit, as he has Jesus mystically proclaiming the Father and Holy Spirit one in unity and purpose, but distinctly different in function. God the Father (Creator), God the Son (Savior and Anointed One), and the Holy Spirit (the power of God's love, the Paraclete), is what we now call Trinitarian belief. It is as if there existed three persons in one deity. From this insightful creation of the early Christian community, the rudimentary form of Trinitarian belief spread. The conviction that there was a God with different functions led to a deity possessing three distinct persons. St Paul constantly invoked this power of the Holy Spirit (the Pentecostal experience) as that which empowered the early Christian community. His use of the blessings of the Holy Spirit is common at the beginning and closing of many of his letters. As the early Christian community began to realize the end of the world (*eschaton*) was not to come exactly as planned, a greater emphasis on the presence of the Holy Spirit became a satisfactory second option for the believer.

Attention to the evolution of the theology of the Holy Spirit is the best way to understand what unique contributions Christ brought to the Jewish world. The immanent presence of God touching every suffering and joyful heart is good news. Personification of this "God presence" is very understandable, since Jesus taught that the outward expression of love in all aspects comes from a believer's heart, not from the Torah or Judaic law. Hence, the idea of a new power and presence is born, a presence unlike anything discussed prior to Jesus.

Beliefs about the Holy Trinity and other such doctrines, formulated after the deaths of the apostles, became the weapons used in many conflicts. Hundreds of verbal and physical wars were fought over the nature of God the Father, the Son of God, and Holy Spirit. All the nonsense edicts that followed simply divided believers into war camps. The ensuing verbal battles after the death of St. Paul persisted, and these battles centered on superfluous matters. In the meantime, the Holy Spirit seems to be very much alive and is a burning flame in every believer's heart. The Father is the expression of power and majesty, just what the ancients, men and women of the Old Testament, called for and believed they would receive. Jesus's function is the bearer of the good news that the old law is about to be fulfilled, as the kingdom is not of a material nature but resides in the heart of the believer. Lastly, the Holy Spirit has come. It is now the duty of Christians to see that further generations recognize the Father, Jesus, and the Holy Spirit in the context of their own personal and changing lives.

The words pronounced in edict and doctrinal forms are really of little concern to the modern Christian believer today. Jesus is the

Son of God the Father (whatever that might mean to us today). The Holy Spirit will always be a riddle in our lives, a conundrum of a relationship between "the other" and ourselves. The need for maintaining the belief of three persons in one God is becoming less meaningful and less credible as a God experience. We will never see the whole picture on this matter of the Trinitarian experience because it does not tell us anything more about God. It is a fabrication of the mind, and no more.

In summary, the possibility of there being a single supreme being with functions instead of persons surfaces as a form of insight into our understanding of God. Believers needed to construct functions to answer both their needs and questions about a God experience. Each function we attribute to God is like that piece of puzzle we alluded to at the beginning of this chapter. Will this puzzle ever be finished? Probably not, as generations in the future will experience a unique God of their own. We hope the believers of the future will have their own pieces of the puzzle to work with for an even clearer image. It is of paramount importance that we look at the Holy Spirit controversies and Trinitarian theologies as an evolving and developing experience. Factions within the early church community led to unfortunate elaborations on the essentials of the God experience. In later chapters, we will look at some of these controversial edicts originating in various communities in the Middle East. At this point, we can garner some idea about the birth of the church. As we see the early Christian community evolving, I believe my statements and conclusions provided are credible. At the same time, they offer an insight into further study as we learn how the power of God's love (the Holy Spirit) inspired the infant Christian church.

3

Changing Some Traditional Starting Points

Back about 1950, I remember my great-uncle telling Dad that the car he bought with an automatic transmission was a big mistake because the vehicle would be too dangerous coming down steep slopes. My dad could lose control at the wheel or burn out his brakes. That kind of car would never sell. My great-uncle never, ever bought anything except a stick shift. I now laugh about it because the San Joaquin valley, where I was born in California, is huge and flat as a pancake, with scarcely a hill in sight for miles. Today, not many buy a standard transmission or even know what it looks like. The point of this story is that all of us change our attitudes constantly, when we find that events and newer ideas and things make much more sense than before. I would like to show how, in our faith, there are times when we need to accommodate and accept a new way of looking at things. The following represent three accommodations necessary for moving our faith forward in today's world. Furthermore, I will tell you why they are important. They are as follows:

1. All religious tenets are unverifiable from a physical point of view.

2. Matter has a radical capacity for life built into its structure.

3. The emergence of *Homo sapiens* takes place without any divine intervention.

God as an Unverifiable Focus for an Act of Faith

For over three thousand years, humankind's idea of God was a revelation of a supreme deity described and defined by ancient leaders, who believed they experienced a real entity. The qualities of this deity were an accepted revelation to individuals (prophets) who possessed great authority, and supposedly accomplished unheralded feats, as long as there was total submission to the commands of the deity. Straying from the dictates revealed to authoritarian leaders resulted in death and destruction to the religious group. There was very little space afforded to the possibility that God was a discovery within, from which humans created certain definite characteristics of an all-knowing, all good, and all-powerful entity. What was certainty of faith at that time was identical with the certainty of fact.

As monotheism developed in ancient Palestine, the focal point for an all-knowing, all good, and all-powerful God centered on one external entity. This belief was an insight transmitted by the prophets of the day. With the onset of Christianity, the sources of belief were some manuscripts, the Torah, and teachings of the early fathers of the church. Once again, there was no room allotted for an idea that humans might be creating a good deal of the attributes of this external God. For the early Christians, the kingdom of God was external, and the risen Christ was soon to come again to establish His kingdom. They paid little attention to the passages in the gospels that indicated a spiritual kingdom originating from one's heart. Repentance and conversion to an external deity were the primary functions of the Christian heart.

With the introduction of science and all the influence it brings to the table, there is a need to forego our traditional belief that God is "out there and verifiable." Note that the word *unverifiable* does not mean the same thing as "nonexistent." It simply means that we just cannot know in faith the way we know things in the tangible world. The questioner needs to consider a supreme being as a discovery of an experience coming from within and unverifiable.

We will not get anywhere, philosophically speaking, by saying a religious revelation comes from outside the human experience. A focus for an act of faith comes from within our hearts and the hearts of a believing community. If we do not take a different orientation, then the questioner with a scientific background can only surmise that, since God is not "out there," He is only a fabrication of the human mind, which is searching for answers to some important matters of life.

I have said that it is important to understand our spiritual beliefs as not physically verifiable. This may be easy to say, but difficult to practice. It involves putting aside our perception of holy objects as spiritually powerful. Secondly, it will require us to revisit such traditionally accepted phenomena as miracles. It is not that miracles cannot be real for us. What it means is that we need to expand the concept of miracles as those experiences bringing us closer to God. We experience the presence of God by our faith, not a physical event. The act of faith is only as real as the power we have to discover God emanating from within ourselves. The act of faith has the same type of reality as love, hate, and the fine arts. Religious beliefs in themselves are always replaceable, but the power of the act of faith, although unverifiable by science, is what persists and keeps us in a relationship with God.

This new view answers questions such as, "On what basis does God choose to heal one person and not the other? If such actions are purely arbitrary, how does this fit in with God being all good?" Unexplainable events constantly happen in the medical field, but they are not called divine interventions or miracles. Science says we just have not figured out all the biological mechanisms that brought about this healing. In fact, the gold standard for drug approval in the pharmaceutical industry is to exceed the placebo effect in drug trials. Unexplainable events happen all the time. It does not mean they will not be verifiable at some point. Because we cannot give physical reasons for an event does not mean it is a divine intervention or miracle.

There are always challenges to changing our convictions. Changes in Christian tenets are extremely slow, compared to common societal changes. Society feels the need to adapt more quickly to a different social, political, or military ideology in the secular world than in religious convictions. Even with the approval of a centralized authority, such as the Roman Catholic Church, alterations of an entrenched belief will find terrific resistance. The status quo is a strong force in traditional religious beliefs; any acceptance of something new and valuable usually takes place slowly, and first at the grassroots level. The challenge to adapt to some novel spiritual ideas does not mean we could not or should not change our convictions.

The problem with the traditional idea of God was that an authority instructed on matters concerning a conviction of faith. Authorities taught that an act of faith was certain and verifiable. There was no difference between faith and reality for a believer.

However, to understand and grasp the value of faith in God today is to examine the faith act as unverifiable. Faith in a deity can still be a real experience, but not measurable in any physical sense. It is within our mind's discovery of God that we give birth to an act of faith and that we actually believe in something. It is upon this insight that we are encouraged to nurture our faith in the future.

Matter Has a Radical Capacity for Life

At this time, it would be good to recall some items we learned in our first year of biology. For those of you not versed in biology, please bear with me as I share some crucial information derived from experiments done over many years. It is important for the reader to draw some credible conclusions from the work already documented through scientific research. Using the term *radical* implies that inanimate matter has, given the right conditions, the ability to form living structures. Once scientists prove this theory, the implications for the presence of *Homo sapiens* could be staggering.

Dr. Stanley Miller (1953) set up an experiment in an attempt to form a number of amino acids, small building blocks of biochemicals, which make up proteins in our body tissue. He placed water vapor, ammonia, and carbon dioxide, all of which are inorganic, into a closed system. After he sent an electric spark (in place of lightning) through these chemicals, thirteen of the twenty to twenty-one essential amino acids spontaneously appeared.[8] Other experiments verified this discovery and the production of protein-like chemicals.[9] As much as some theorists question whether early Earth's conditions were as Miller had suggested, no one has ever denied the validity of the experiment. Given the right conditions, science has shown how simple inorganic molecules form larger and more complex chemical structures resembling biochemicals. Courtney Humphries, in an article in *Harvard Magazine*, shared an intriguing insight from Martin Nowak that evolution is really the driver of life formation. This movement forward culminates in the formation of the fundamental proteins (ribonucleotides), thought to be the initial structures in the reproductive process billions of years ago. What is implied in the article is that scientific interest is not so much in the origins of life as in the steps and processes as evolution takes place.[10]

The point of these two initial references is to show how, using simple organic chemicals, nature appears to have the capacity to give rise to the complex molecules found in all living tissues. Of course, it is still a major leap to say life has come from nonlife. Biochemicals are not biology. Most scientists in the field maintain that small coacervates (membranous structures formed under laboratory conditions) resemble living cells that existed in the primordial soup of our oceans. Scientists have not at present come to an agreement on just how and where in the earth's primitive ocean such a breakthrough occurred. From single cells, the rest of the story about our biological presence is an ongoing effort undertaken by dedicated research scientists. At this time, no one has received the Nobel Prize for laboratory efforts at creating a living cell from nonliving components. Years ago, the media over-exaggerated an announcement by Arthur Kornberg (1918–2007) that he had successfully created life in a test tube. In fact, he had engineered the production of a strand of DNA from components taken from previously existing genetic structures. Regardless of one's opinion on the matter, a genetic strand of DNA created in a test tube must be able to replicate again many times, and this did not happen.[11] However, Kornberg and his son should be extolled for their monumental work in discovering the enzymes that played essential roles in the replication of the genetic strands in living organisms.

From single cells to complex organisms, such as *Homo sapiens,* science has discovered patterns of behavior that become more sophisticated as we move up the tree of life. Small cellular organisms adapt to a colonial environment in which it is more likely to achieve the drive for survival. As cells take on a colonial structure, for the same reason do larger organisms find such processes beneficial for survival of species. This means that cells begin to take on specific functions in the process of ingesting food, respiration, reproduction, and other life functions. Over the millions of years that it takes to achieve these novel ways to live, a pattern of relationships begins to surface. Certain cells take on a function that contributes to the benefit of the larger structure as well as the single-celled structure. The implication is that, as the cellular structure becomes more complex, biologists are able to identify patterns of more complex behavior and predict that these patterns of behavior will occur.

Differentiation has occurred to the extent that one type of cell becomes dependent on the others for survival within that organism. From simple cellular structures, there appear tissues and organs forming a complex organism. Not all cells will achieve this level. It can be demonstrated that some cells have incorporated such specialization to the point that they carry the genetics of that organism for only the purpose of reproduction, while other cells, although carrying the genetic code, are not at all involved in the reproductive process. Specialization and differentiation of cells within an organism will become a product of environmental pressures as well as a genetically determined process.

The evolutionary development, up the tree of life to primates, is much more sophisticated than outlined here, but the idea is clear. In complex organisms, the relationship between cells, tissues, and organs is such that scientists can observe something similar to a city functioning for survival. Cells function for the greater good of the organism, as well as survival for themselves. In fact, contributing to the greater good of the organism ensures the overall survival of that cell's existence in the evolutionary process. What I am leading up to is the reader's acceptance of an insight that matter—inorganic, organic, and biochemical—exhibits a capacity for generating not only a living cell, but ultimately complex living structures as well. According to scientists, this progress occurs without intervention of any kind other than the evolutionary process. Now the question is, how can this discussion apply to *Homo sapiens*? How does one move from animal consciousness to human consciousness without an intervention of some kind? An acceptance of this topic is essential for moving in a direction that can satisfy the inquiring mind.

The Emergence of *Homo Sapiens*

Keep in mind that, although the processes for the production of life began billions of years ago, *Homo sapiens* has only recently appeared. For the genus *Homo,* this would be a fraction of time within an evolutionary development of several million years. What were simple relationships in the more primitive animals have become extremely complex behavioral relationships, built up to ensure the survival of a species. As it does today, survival depended on the existence of a community relationship. Groups, clans, and tribes stayed together for survival, just as contemporary lower mammals do today. What we need to discuss now is how nature arrived at human intelligence and self-consciousness. Explanations as to the emergence of *Homo sapiens* are very fundamental and possibly oversimplified in this work. Nonetheless, since this work is not a science textbook, it is important to keep the thoughts on a level to which a non–professional scientist can relate. Anthropologists will agree that humankind's emergence on earth was a very complex and detailed combination of processes. These processes appeared through random genetic changes in the gene pool and through the ability of groups to educate the population in the best way to survive, given certain adaptive characteristics.

There are morphological (physical) traits that probably set the scene for the emergence of humans. Anthropologists have listed many of these traits. The following are of note: upright position, taillessness, binocular vision, opposable thumbs, integrated and walking hind legs and feet, increasingly hairless bodies, omnivorous dental structure, and enlarged endocranial capacity. Associated with the development of the human mind is the disproportionately large brain in comparison to the size of the body. Furthermore, the cerebral cortex (seat of thought) is disproportionately larger than the other portions of the brain. One could address other human physical traits. Though these physical traits may not be the most important characteristics, they do set the scene for the emergence of behavioral characteristics. These characteristics will definitely set *Homo sapiens* apart as a special species, different from other primates.

The unique qualities of what we define as human intelligence and consciousness require consideration. This is a type of activity which sets *Homo sapiens* above and apart from other primates. We are the only species that can self-direct, self-reflect, determine its own future, and construct complex societies exhibiting ethical, religious, and artistic prowess. Scientists believe these accomplishments developed for purposes of insuring survival of a human population. Our species has ascended out of and away from a simple innate behavior, which means it allows us to be astoundingly creative in producing structures and products from the goods of the earth. This behavior results in not just more and larger products but essentially different products.

Although we share over 95 percent of our DNA with lower primates, the difference in DNA is important, and this difference has resulted in unparalleled feats in biological history. Science assumes a polygenetic origin of the human species. We understand there were several distinct groups of humanlike primates inhabiting the trees and living on the savannahs in Africa. Darwinian principles came into play here as a way of weeding out primitive humanlike forms less likely to survive when foraging for food and competing for territory.

It is a credible assumption that when a major portion of the key morphological characteristics are in place, characteristics described as human begin to appear in the gene pool. What we know is that human activity appears as a natural phenomenon arising out of interaction on different levels for the survival of the population. Scientists admit this is not an entirely verifiable discovery, but studies done in primate research find a remarkable similarity to human behavior taking place. Without going into detail on the question of the emergence of humans, one can readily assume as correct most key conclusions reached by anthropologists today.

The challenge for science today is to show that all human activity is the result of the evolution of physiological changes, above and beyond those found in lower primates. Science has not shown from actual, verifiable data that our activity reduces itself to neural and electrochemical activity in our brains. This would be unverifiable, even though, when looking at the whole picture of human development, the tendency is to say our human nature originates from an extraordinary evolutionary novelty.

It is at this point of the discussion that religion can actually lay claim to certain tenets with just as much certainty as science. The tendency, I admit, is for the scientist to say God and religious matters are totally a fabrication of the mind. This would be a gross assumption, since I have maintained that faith in God is an act of discovery and not just a manmade construct to control behavior in a population.

Pertaining to human intelligence and consciousness, at this time, scientific research simply has not shown any more certainty of fact in the matter than religion has shown certainty of faith. Both domains are unverifiable as to the source of what it means to be human. I say this just as I would say the same about the difference between an enclosed assortment of biochemicals and an actual functioning cell. From a theological point of view, what is important for the modern Christian to admit is that continued research into the machinations of the brain could only increase an understanding of and appreciation for humans' emergence. Scientists are sure that in the not-too-distant future, they will be able to verify the emergence of humans without resorting to any divine intervention. Our faith must accommodate to this discovery.

The purpose of this chapter has been to point out what I believe needs to be incorporated into our belief system. I cited three examples of how we can move forward in the evolution of our belief system. The insight that God is an unverifiable yet real focus for our act of faith, and does not function in a physical manner, would be an essential admission we have to make. Secondly, that matter has the capacity to create complexities not unlike life, without any intervention. Finally, the evolutionary development of *Homo sapiens* in its entirety is a fact. We need to move ahead with these insights and determine how they can support our beliefs. One may suggest there are other focal points requiring a consensus for moving a Christian perspective ahead. However, without a doubt, the future act of faith will need these three items for balancing one's belief with the contributions of science.

4

Revisiting Some Treasured Religious Concepts

As a teen, I found pulling nails from used constructions boards to be a disgusting task. Our wood-burning stove was very hungry in winter months. The task was not a pleasant memory for me while living on the farm. Nevertheless, there were many fond memories from childhood that are worth revisiting. Upon looking back at my reactions to some important doctrines of faith, I realize I had an admitted acceptance of anything taught. As my pastor and religion teachers spoke about religious history, doctrines, and beliefs, I accepted what the spiritual teachers said as the truth. Confidence and security were strong because someone else thought for me. However, life is different today. As adults, we need to think for ourselves. Some treasured beliefs are like thorny and painful nails. We need to pull out these convictions to find the important and relevant precepts beneath, for preserving the legacy Christ passed on to His followers.

In this chapter, I would like to take a few basic beliefs and see how they might fit into a Christian perspective now and for the future. I have chosen three basic doctrines very much alive today. They are the creation, incarnation, and redemption. These beliefs are like construction boards with nails needing to be pulled.

Creation

Science tells us that our universe today is the result of both slow and rapid cataclysmic events occurring over some fourteen billion years. I believe many people are not satisfied with a nonscientific biblical approach to explaining our universe as it exists today. Presently, we have, on the one hand, what religious tradition espouses and on the other, what science has demonstrated—all contained in one box of beliefs. In the end, the traditional stance does nothing except to relegate creation to the level of myth. There should be much more to creation, from a religious point of view, for future generations to accept as a valid item of belief. At this point, two questions are appropriate. What does creation mean? Secondly, can creation be a valid form of belief with something for everyone to consider relevant today?

It should not be a shock to know that there are ways to look at creation other than how religious institutions have understood the concept in Christian tradition. The belief system that holds creation as something coming to be from nothing is very restrictive, yet most Christians have that precise understanding. Even in Genesis, the use of "formless void," and "darkness over the deep," does not mean "nothing." The second account of creation in Genesis automatically assumes the presence of matter,[12] but this second account does not usually appear in today's liturgical events. Does something really come from nothing? The author of Genesis would not have been able to ask, let alone answer, this question. The modern theology of creation assumes a philosophy the Hebrews simply did not have.[13]

There is a deep consensus among theologians that the biblical story of the origin of the cosmos is not a scientific work, although some sects still maintain a literal acceptance of the book of Genesis. We know there is no room in the educated mind for a seven-day feat of divine intervention. There are other stories of our origin from ancient times and cultures, but it is not necessary to discard this story, since it is such a beautiful and tremendously inspiring narrative. St. Thomas Aquinas hinted at the need to solve this issue, in that he espoused the possibility that matter could be eternal. However, in his own inimitable way, he was more intent on constructing the levels of creation than delving into creation out of nothing. In modern times, we have had great minds understanding creation in Genesis as something beyond that taught by institutional religion.

We need to be aware that ancient Hebrew thought was confronting Mesopotamian myth, which espoused that out of the spirit of chaos, godlike beings emerged from nothing. What it has in common with pagan myth is the implication of the presence of water in the "darkness over the deep." Albert Einstein, although a professed pantheist, spoke of creation in a much different manner, although some thought his understanding to be still somewhat traditionally religious when he said, "God does not play dice with the universe."[14] Stephen Hawking has done extensive work on the origin of the universe. He was somewhat amused when both Pope John Paul II and Pope Benedict XVI thought the term *creation* used by Hawking was similar to their own understanding of creation as a traditional religious belief.[15] Hawking does not understand creation in the sense of a creative act of God, but rather, how the universe came to be without divine intervention, i.e., the big bang theory.

Without going into the details of a modern scientific explanation of the big bang theory, we can say that one cannot dispel the enduring quality of three correlated yet different realities: energy, matter, and space/time. None of these realities can exist without the other. For instance, space/time can be minimized to what we call nothingness, yet could still exist because it can be the product of the interaction of energy and matter in a tumultuous reaction. We can say the same of the other two realities. Einstein's equation even indicates the inter-convertibility between energy and matter ($E = mc^2$) at one point in the space/time continuum. Furthermore, all three realities could conceivably exist in a parallel universe and/or oscillating universe (multiple big bangs). This is what I believe is the modern scientific explanation of a creative act. Out of a monstrous big black hole comes the birth of these three recognizable realities. In fact, experimentations with the Large Hadron Collider in Europe continually explain, or at least illustrate, how the creative act of the universe could be achieved. Scientists have predicted and evidently identified the building block of all matter and have called it the God particle (Higgs boson). The reader will notice that creation does not fit the traditional ideas expressed by religions.

Modern belief systems must adapt to the amazing discoveries of science in order for the believer to move ahead with what the creative act of God means in his or her life. My attempt at this point is not to explain the origin of the universe, but to offer the possibility of bridging the present knowledge of science with a belief system that includes God as creator or originator. A belief system need not relinquish the richness of a faith tradition because science has seriously called into question the validity of a story of creation. At this point in our evolutionary history, faith and science are not the same. The domains are different, the tools are different, and the methodologies are different. What the believer needs to know is that it is possible to incorporate the wonders of science into a belief system without discarding the story of creation as untrue. To accomplish this task requires the expansion of one's belief system. I can believe a story in Genesis to be true and at the same time know that the story is not a chapter out of a science book. It is an admission, for the first time, that the creative act of God can be understood in new ways. The biblical expressions on creation in Genesis have a value as myths with a moral. We should not try to move these myths into physical reality. Is the acceptance of God as the ultimate creative act enough to accept? If matter in the universe is eternal, we may never know what the ultimate creative act means. However, we are continually learning more about creation through the achievements of science.

The use of the word *creation* can no longer be simply the domain of a religious belief system; it is also, with recent discoveries, a functional term readily used by cosmologists and philosophers as well. Neither the Bible nor religious institutional beliefs can hold a domain or copyright on the concept of creation. Scientists generally have no affiliation with a belief system on creation.

The intricacies of what happens in the universe's creative act must not upset us, even if the understanding of these details may change. If faith is a real experience in our lives, then we must continually look at and pray for an understanding of the bigger picture. As far as scientists are concerned, creation is still taking place, and the eternal interaction of matter and energy is the very nature of this universe. We need to question, in the traditional sense, whether God is someone out there, or rather the creative act we discover not with instruments, but in our very hearts. We can create the presence of God when we live out His good news in our lives, and we can say we have just pulled a few nails from the creation board!

The Incarnation

Deeply imbedded in early Christian tradition is the conviction that God was made human, came upon the earth in a very mysterious way, lived as the flesh of humans lives, grew in mind and body as humans grow in mind and body, suffered as any human feels suffering, and finally died. Yet, from the beginning of Jesus's public life and well into the second century, no one really understood the implication of what all of this means. Believers believed what preachers preached; spiritual leaders put doctrines on the table; and all believers had to believe or leave. Put in today's context, and relevant to the knowledge and understanding expected today, how can we look back and not ask serious questions about the God-human phenomenon? If a modern inquirer were to investigate this thing called incarnation, he could easily say to someone that it would have been good to do a DNA test on Jesus at the time. Yes, and where would one think that the Y chromosome originated? Since God is pure act and not material in any manner, we should be looking for someone down in the village for answers to this question. Joseph, the stepfather, was himself probably pondering the same question, but, as tradition says, he was prepared to quietly take Mary under his own care and raise a family together with this young virgin, or at least quietly divorce her. It was not important to the early disciples whether Mary was a virgin or had other children. Why is this so? It is because that was not an issue at the time. However, by the end of the first century, numerous theological pundits attempted to convince the believing community that Jesus was of divine origin and not conceived naturally.

It is my belief that controversies about Jesus as Son of God were the cause of later church statements on this topic. The early writings of Jesus's disciples simply showed no interest in this aspect of Jesus's origin, only that Jesus was the son of a carpenter, Son of God, and carried the force of the promised Messiah in His words and deeds. The incarnation narrative found in St. Luke's gospel uses Old Testament quotes to show to the Jewish community a connection between Jesus and the promised Messiah, the fulfill-ment of the predictions found in the Torah, the prophets, and the other manuscripts available at the time.

Centuries of growth of the Christian church resulted in a picture of a material kingdom to be managed (i.e., the papacy), rather than the immaterial kingdom of the Father, which, as Jesus con-tinually said, existed in the hearts of the believers. To explain how and why distortions took place over the centuries will take a few pages. Please bear with me as I move into a brief explanation as to how and to what extent deviation from the original words of Jesus took place. In the next chapter, I will treat in more detail the science that attempts to explain deviations in sacred texts.

In St. John's prologue to his gospel, the appearance of the "Word of God" occurs. In the remaining writings of St. John, reference to Jesus as the Word of God is noticeably absent. We have no idea if this is an alteration, redaction, or insertion by a later writer, and this is unfortunate. In the Greek language, beautiful imagery flows from the nature of the *logos* (word as voice) to Jesus pitching his tent among men (word as act). In the Old Testament, the Word of God is simply a voice speaking, not an act "happening." It is unfortunate that the author did not expand and explore the word in more detail. When the "Word was made flesh" (act happening), it was enough for St. John to think about it on the spiritual and experiential level, without allowing for a distinction of both the spiritual and physical presence. What I mean by this is that there is the expression of a god (spiritual), and human (physical), but not an explanation of the unity of the two entities. What likely happened is that John was not aware of a problem and simply only looked at it on the spiritual and experiential level. In my opinion, a simple explanation would be that Jesus was born a man and at His baptism became the Son of God, as we are all called to be sons and daughters of God. This would be a difficult nail to pull from the incarnation board.

Unfortunately, over the decades following John's death, people introduced various personal spiritual interpretations, causing factions and alienations, resulting in synods and councils that attempted to define in doctrinal form what it was that had to be believed. A formal creed explaining what was to be believed and taught was issued after a debate at the Council of Nicaea (325 CE), altered again in 381 CE at the council of Constantinople, and lastly at the Council of Toledo in 589 CE. Most believe that a concurrent Apostles' Creed (not related to the disciples of Christ, only named as such) predated the Nicene Creed by forty to fifty years but only became commonly used near the end of the fourth century. Historical theologians may differ on what creed was considered more important, but none can deny that the understanding of the early fathers, and consequently the common faithful, certainly evolved by adapting to the challenges of the time. Wars and imprisonments rose out of concepts related to the incarnation. The actual birth of Christ narratives represent innovative approaches in an attempt to attract and inspire believers and probably bear little resemblance to what actually happened. We do know that the intent of New Testament scripture was to show the common Jew that the Messiah foretold in Isaiah and elsewhere became reality in the incarnation. However, the teachings of the early disciples refer to none of the intricate incarnation narratives.

After the death of the first disciples, the decades following witnessed a Diaspora of the Jewish community and the conversion of Gentiles (non-Jews) throughout the Middle East. Beliefs centering on the nature of Jesus, God the Father, and the Holy Spirit developed very much as expected and relied on the knowledge transmitted by the disciples and the education of the newly converted. What developed quickly were many verbal controversies. In the Acts of the Apostles, St. Paul and others in their letters were constantly attempting to manage differences of beliefs in the newly formed communities. Questions about the good news and saving mercy of Jesus become questions about the Word of God made flesh, the Son of God being human and God, the person of Jesus being equal to the person of the Paraclete (Holy Spirit), who was on the same footing as God the Father. With the crowning of Constantine as the first Christian emperor of Rome, less emphasis was placed on the Word of God than what was *meant* by the Word of God (His voice). Prior to this time, there was no church state. Local churches were still autonomous in their preaching. With the ecclesiastical shift to Rome, there was much more insistence upon uniformity. This shift within the power of state (union of the Catholic Church into the Holy Roman Empire) eventually led to the great schism in the eleventh century.

The first five councils, starting with the council of Nicaea (325 CE), recount differences of thought about the incarnated God and attempts by bishops (theologians of the time) exacerbated the problem by inventing new explanations with more defined and esoteric language. Elaboration upon the verbal controversies was more important than breaking bread together and praying over the common elements of belief found in localized manuscripts. Later councils deliberated on the nature of the Eucharist. Although there were numerous challenges in each of the councils, I will focus on edicts that relate to the incarnate God.

The Council of Nicaea (325 CE) promulgated the "consubstantiality" of the Holy Spirit with the Son of God and with the heavenly Father. That term was invented to help explain why the doctrine of the Trinity must be a mandated belief. The church will admit that this Trinitarian concept is neither explainable nor based on reason. However, (God) as father, (God) as son and brother, and God the Holy Spirit (the relationship between Son and Father) could be credible to a Christian believer. We can now understand God as "one" with distinct functions in time. The believer should take refuge in a supreme being for what that means within a faith experience.

The Council of Ephesus (431 CE), among other things, declared divine maternity. What that means is Jesus was born with two natures, divine and human, but still, in accordance with the previous council, remains just one person who is divine. At this time, the development of personhood obscured function (discussed in the previous chapter), and the unity of one God with various functions was lost forever.

At the time of the **Council of Chalcedon (451 CE),** a growing schism between the Roman communities and the communities of Asia Minor was apparent. Condemnation of any sects that held the unity of the single nature of Christ resulted in a contentious problem which did not have to exist. A power shift was showing up, and the power of a political state was probably involved. It was not a question of agreeing to disagree for the sake of the simplicity of belief, but rather the insistence on adherence to the supremacy and declarations of the theater (performance) of the mind.

The Second Council of Constantinople (553 CE) declared that heresy was running rampant regarding edicts issued at previous councils. There existed in Asia Minor many renditions of the books of the New Testament that were not in line with apostolic tradition and with the letters from the early disciples. There were also several other gospels preached that later became part of the eastern Christian church's beliefs.

The Third Council of Constantinople (681 CE) was actually called by Emperor Constantine IV because of the apparent threat of Islam. Further condemnations were promulgated relating to the nature of Christ's will. In my opinion, it is simply inconceivable how anybody has anything to say about Christ's will, whether divine or human.

The Fourth Council of Constantinople (869 CE) resulted in the closure of all Latin churches in Asia Minor. Attempts at reconciliation were to no avail, and by the eleventh century, the schism between East and West was complete. Rome was declared the papal seat of Peter. Ecumenical councils followed in the quest to solidify operational matters within the Holy Roman Empire. Continual condemnation of heretical teachings occurred, and elimination of antipopes took place. The Roman Catholic power shift to Rome was complete.

The Fourth Lateran Council (1215 CE) set in stone the term *transubstantiation* relating to the doctrine of the real presence of Jesus "confected" into the body and blood of Jesus in the Eucharist. Power now centered on the priest and his function relating to the sacraments. For all practical purposes, matters relating to the incarnation and what theologians thought up were now set in stone. A preponderance of verbiage and edicts had permanently split nations apart from a simple and holy devotion to the Word (the voice of God) incarnate. All this was due to intellectualizing theologians and philosophers.

Some historians call the Middle Ages, leading up to the Reformation in the sixteenth century, the Dark Ages. Tumultuous conditions resulted in a corrupt papacy, trying to exist under the cruel fingers of warring political states, and, of course, the scourge of the Black Death (bubonic plague), that took almost half the population of western Europe. With the onset of the printing press (early fifteenth century), extensive effort was made to maintain the status quo on dogmatic proclamations. The marriage of the state to the papacy was solidified in the tenth century (during the Holy Roman Empire), and this condition persisted through the Renaissance up to the time of the Augustinian monk, Martin Luther, and even into the nineteenth century.

The theater of the mind had complete dominance until the Second Vatican Council in 1962. The products of the mind distorted simple beliefs, and the defense of these products was even more contorted. The Catholic Church has innumerable volumes of senseless edicts that accomplish nothing except distrust, alienation, and controversy. Emperors fought battles and took over kingdoms. Popes were banished over senseless arguments about matters of the incarnation. Scholars can document the history of the Word incarnate, but few wish to discuss how the evolution of this Christian belief took place. It was not under the inspiration of the Holy Spirit, but rather due to the machinations of intellectual tomfoolery and the desire for power. No one went back to the ancient Hebrew belief that the voice of God was His Word, not his act. It was believed that in becoming flesh, the Word of God had reached its fulfillment in the Christ figure, the longings of the prophets. I believe we can understand the incarnation better as God's Word embodied in a Christ figure. Furthermore, just as Christ is the Word of God, so also God calls all men and women to be His Word. We are essentially brothers and sisters of the human Christ, and, like Christ, we are sons and daughters of God. When we love one another, as Christ taught us to do, we become God's voice to humankind.

In summary, if one considers all aspects of the incarnation, it becomes clear that theological thoughts and consequent practices evolved a great deal during the first six centuries. Such changes were not simply refining measures. Major theological turnarounds took place. When there were few manuscripts and many believers were illiterate, one would expect such things to occur. By the advent of the Council of Nicaea and later councils of the time, bishops defined what the Holy Spirit and the word of God meant, and made initial mistakes regarding the insistence that the Holy Spirit divinely inspired the writers of the Holy Scripture. Changes to the sacred writings occurred continually, and with the Synod at Rome in 382 CE, the twenty-seven books of the New Testament became formally accepted with all their alterations and modifications.

The holy writers of the time may have been inspired, but not divinely inspired. As early as 367 CE, the twenty-seven canonical writings were extolled by St. Athanasius, with respect given to the apocrypha, which were described as other contributions worthy of reading. By the year 500 CE, the church ecclesiastically defined and accepted the official canon of the New Testament. With the advent of monasticism (the first seminary began earlier, about 180 CE), scribes and other devoted monks took to the task of writing manuscripts for communities around the Middle East. A brief history of the early councils of the church helps put a perspective to the challenges the institutional church faced as the Christian faith spread throughout Asia Minor and finally into Rome. The controversies regarding the nature of Christ constituted just a portion of the animosity that developed between the Holy Roman Church and the Eastern Church, now called the Orthodox Church.

The Redemption

Considering the three Christian concepts being treated in this chapter, the concept of redemption is by far the belief that has evolved and been developed the most slowly. The passion, death, and resurrection form the historical fabric of our redemption. The Christian experiences a need for a Messiah, a savior, and some kind of immortality. As Christians, we will never drop these from our experience of the historical Jesus. Since my early days, I have never forgotten two acclamations, often repeated while praying through the ritual of the Stations of the Cross. I will address the issue of redemption from these two prayers that, in this chapter, will take on new meanings. The first is as follows:

> We adore you, O Christ, and we bless you, because through your death and resurrection you have redeemed the world.

With the Adam and Eve tradition containing the seeds of the fall of humanity from grace and innocence, we can initiate a discussion on the matter of redemption. Most educators in science maintain the story of the fall of Adam to be a myth, with a possible moral. We can say the same about the other four mythic instances of the fall of humanity. There is a limitation to how much a myth can intrude into the world of reality and science. Acceptance by science of the polygenetic origin of humanity has required theologians to rethink these stories as an ideal tool for teaching important moral principles. If this is the case, then one has to limit the relevance of original sin to the whole matter of redemption. It is one thing to say that we all share in the nature of Adam and Eve as our mythic parents, and another thing to say that they were our real parents who were thrown out of paradise. In fact, the Catholic Church still upholds Adam and Eve as our real parents, without taking into account the insights that many of her own theologians have offered. It does not make any difference how one might interpret St. Paul's Letter to the Romans 5:12, where St. Paul states: "Sin entered the world through one man, and through sin death, and thus death has spread through the whole human race *because*[16] everyone has sinned." The concept of original sin is still understood to be "actual" in a real Adam, though a "habit" (vice) in humans. In other words, all men and women possess the vice of the sin of a first parent called Adam.

The Adam and Eve Myth Goes Viral

Although there is no transmission of sin mentioned in the Adam story, the myth is now an entrance point for explaining why sin is here. Consequently, we are educated in the belief that we are "fallen" from birth. Most theologians maintain original sin because humans have sinned and are sinners (and I add the comment as I did earlier in this work—"humankind therefore needs God"). There has to be a reason why Christ went through all this suffering: we just had to be redeemed.

Original sin is a sin of collectivity, a sin in all humankind, in that we are all brought into the community of human beings. Redemption by Christ means that all of humanity has been "bought back" from this collective sin. This is not the same as salvation. Individuals are saved, and all of humanity is redeemed. As the church understands and promotes the concept, we participate in an ungraced community at birth. We work out our salvation in the course of our lives. Finally, with this reasoning, personal sin ratifies the first sin. Some theologians have proposed that, once conscience appears, we share in the fallen nature of humanity. Certainly, there are critics who take issue with each of the above discussions on the fall of humanity, but this theology of the sinfulness of humanity is a move ahead. Now it is imperative that creative thought move ahead with what these ideas propose.

For many centuries, theological thought formed a quagmire of stubbornness and refusal to take a new stance and stand by it. A possible explanation for the Catholic Church's or other denominations' refusal to move ahead with a creative look at redemption is because the rejection of Genesis as factual leads to serious challenges. The dismissal of the Adam and Eve story as anything more than myth calls into question the event of the fall, which dismisses original sin and the reason for Christ's passion and death being a redemptive act. If theologians insist that redemption is necessarily dependent on the traditional fall of humanity, there is a time in the near future when a rude awakening must take place. Once again, someone should offer a quiet suggestion that we are risen primates, rather than fallen angels.[17] We are at first individuals who are conscious to differing degrees, and then, with education in a community, we form a conscience from experience, learning what it means to sin within a population of humans.

> Lord, by your cross and resurrection you have set
> us free; you are the Savior of the world.

This prayer is a beautiful expression of the community of faith, its acceptance of the Holy Triduum (Easter) as a devotional time, and a purposeful experience of Jesus as our redeemer. It is important at this point to look at a bigger picture of the redemptive act of Jesus. I think we ought to include the incarnation as part a saving action in our regard, as well. The transcendent broke into our reality with total embodiment, in such a way as we have yet to comprehend. Most of the old mysteries carrying over from Old Testament concepts no longer provide an answer to the challenges of faith and only provide inspirational reading. New Testament accounts (including the gospels, Acts of the Apostles, and epistles) will always present to us a partial understanding of the redemptive act of Christ. These manuscripts are time- and context-restricted, falling out of relevance in our time. Instead of pulling us out of a proverbial pit of sin, death, and darkness, redemption needs to include an act of invitation, a call to pursue what it means to be redeemed as we discover ourselves in the future. We must look ahead to what redemption means for humanity and not be content to look back and see what it has done for us. We need to explore further what it could mean to be "set free," in the words of the acclamation.

What It Means to Be Free

Have you ever stuck a pin into an inflated balloon or burst a large bubble with your finger? The surge of air and the following reaction of astonishment make it really worth doing over again. The pressure inside of the balloon has been released, exploding into the surrounding air. Similarly, traditional religion has by its nature exerted a tie-down effect *(religion* in Latin means to be bound to something), fastening the believer to a list of dictates or a system of beliefs. What it can now mean for the future believer is liberation from the complex institutional dictates and the needless theological definitions of medieval times into a life of discovery of what God can mean for us today.

The simplicity and freshness of being "liberated" from a personal habitual sinfulness allows a discovery of what redemption can be for the Christian now and in the future. In his letter to the Romans, St. Paul speaks of this, but with a different intent, when he discusses freedom from the law. Explosion into the reality of knowing we are "sons and daughters of God" (as Jesus proclaimed to be the good news) means something much more than taking on redemption as understood during the first centuries of Christianity. We take on the personality of Christ as Christ is for modern times, not for what Christ was. A discussion on the evolution of the term *Messiah* is pertinent at this point.

Up to about the second century BCE, the understanding of *Messiah* (anointed one and deliverer) was very clear. Having been through at least two catastrophic exiles, the Israelites longed for a home. The restoration of the kingdom of David to the chosen people was a top-priority belief. More than once, Jesus had to respond to these insistent and nagging questions: "Will you restore our kingdom back to us? Will I be able to sit with you on your right hand?" Jesus's response, of course, was through parables and analogies, and the people still did not understand, Even His close disciples did not understand. Their tradition did not include immortality, let alone the concept of a spiritual kingdom. Immortality was the amorphous idea of living on in one's progeny, which, if one was lucky, would "number as the stars."[18] When Jesus said, "My kingdom is not of this world,"[19] spiritual dimensions other than what the Greek and Roman beliefs offered were not conceivable. According to the apostles, the resurrected Jesus was to return and gather His people up in the "end time," and the dissolution of the world would occur. It is possible for us to get a glimpse of what the early disciples understood the Messiah to be as we look carefully at the scenes of the baptism of Jesus, the glorification of Jesus on the mountain, and the ascension. The voice from heaven, the appearance of Christ with Moses and Elijah, and the ascending of Jesus up into the sky, after which an angel told the people to go home, are definitely postresurrection narratives. All of these clearly indicate some kind of material kingdom over which Jesus exercises dominion. That the new kingdom of God was from within did not really register, although Jesus did talk about it. A theology of the Messiah definitely evolved before long into a conviction that Jesus, as Messiah, suffered and died for the sins of many. Jesus is the promised Messiah. Jesus is the redeemer who saves us from our sins. That He will gather all His faithful ones is a revelation persisting as something new, and so, such a belief continues to this day. It is my belief that we must improve these traditional concepts as we move into the future. We must allow the saving actions of Jesus to move forward.

In summary, the idea of what it means to be redeemed in theology needs serious reworking with the relegation of the fall of Adam and Eve to the level of myth by today's modern Christians. Original sin and being born into sinfulness are concepts needing serious changes. Precisely how we bring this about is not clear, but we need to accommodate to new insights for moving forward. Questions need to be asked and answered as to what relevance traditional understandings offer about creation, the incarnated Word, and redemption today. The voice of God is the Word. The Word is a liberating experience because it is an invitation to seek further into the meaning of the kingdom existing in our hearts. Redemption is more like an invitation to a new way of living in the future, not the past. To be risen with Christ is expanding our understanding (like the air in a balloon) to greater insights of what creation, incarnation, and redemption have in store for us.

Looking at the construction boards filled with nagging nails (discussed at the beginning of this chapter), we are preserving the wood for the future. In the same way, we treasure the tradition the early fathers have provided, knowing that it is time to develop what has been given to us for a more meaningful and holy future.

5

Textual Criticism, an Inside Look

I will never forget the delightful movie *Lost in Translation* (2003), with Bill Murray in the leading role. In the movie, there was always an expectation that the two main characters would finally come together with a melodramatic ending for the viewer. That did not happen, and several reasons surface in the viewer's mind. Was the outcome really due to something lost in translation? One might think that language was the main culprit, because of a difference in ethnic background (the movie takes place in Tokyo), but that was not the case. Instead, it seems to be a classic case of hesitation and misunderstanding between the main character and another man's wife. We see the first failure in communication when an interpreter tries to explain to Bill Murray (Bob) in English what the director of the commercial is saying and wants done. The viewer of the movie gets the impression there is much more being lost in translation than just the filming of a commercial. Nonetheless, it was an entertaining movie. The subject matter of this chapter treats some possible misunderstandings and items that go beyond just the translation of languages for the sake of communication. At this point, the purpose is to show how the science of textual criticism of the Bible adds a huge component to our understanding of the evolution of Christian belief. I hope that the reader's attention is not lost in my translation of ideas.

One of the most difficult and scholarly endeavors in literary research is not only to explore deeper meanings of phrases in historical documents, but also to investigate the altered meanings and authenticity of literary pieces. Biblical scholars in the last two centuries have excelled in their intensive and painstaking analysis of manuscripts available from the first five centuries. The Roman Catholic Church is the main preserver of the early Christian manuscripts, yet real critical work appeared after the Reformation. Restrictions on Catholic theologians after Luther limited the scope of study to spiritual and pastoral themes. The past two centuries exhibited an amazing amount of research done by Protestant and other non-Catholic biblical scholars. Textual criticism, along with other forms of criticism, became an authentic form of research resulting in insights into early Christian beliefs and practices. The early fathers of the church were intent on controlling the proliferation of manuscripts in Egypt and Asia Minor. The city of Alexandria, during the third and fourth centuries, produced the most accurate copies of Holy Scripture.[20] At the time of Saint Irenaeus, the early church attempted to refute supposed heretics who became quite influential among the eastern churches. Each eastern community produced manuscripts that differed slightly, depending on what a spiritual leader was preaching at the time. Most of the early manuscripts were written by unprofessional scribes bent on reflecting differences of opinion on topics such as multiple gods, Christ's nature as divine and human, and heretical Trinitarian beliefs.[21]

During the first four centuries, the prelates were very determined to prevent heretics from using a text to promote a heretical point of view. They condoned changes to an original manuscript, changes that would eliminate the possibility of getting the wrong idea about what the apostles and the early disciples believed to be Jesus's nature and message.

Contemporary textual criticism entails more than deciphering what was the original text in a story; it also looks into how and why a modification took place. In modern times, the Catholic Church places restrictions upon its scholars in their approach to open research and methodology. Prelates instruct Catholic scholars that there is a full inspiration and inerrant nature attached to all the sacred writings of Holy Scripture. The Catholic Church accepts the works of non-Catholic critics, as long as conclusions do not contradict the established dogmatic teaching of the church. God insured the truth of scripture by the grace of His inspiration. This kind of thinking makes it very difficult to work in biblical studies when the Bible is considered to be divinely inspired and the writers to be instruments of the Holy Spirit. An inquirer is not able to contact the Holy Spirit to find out what happened and why it happened. To challenge a univocal statement by the Catholic Church means to challenge its doctrinal statements and infallibility.

All Catholic scholars must work with three parameters set down for studying Holy Scripture. First, the Bible is the word of God that proclaims a divine lesson. Second, an inspired text cannot err. Third, the Bible is free from error and is beyond all doubt the teaching of apostolic tradition. Contemporary theologians object to these restrictions, which prevent a full examination of the text from an unbiased point of view. Such restrictions also inhibit a more scientific attempt at studying scripture.

I will briefly discuss just a few examples of alterations by the mainline church. These alterations eventually led down a path resulting in the Catholic doctrine we have to this day. In short, these examples represent just a few of many changes that determined the direction of Christian belief at a time when apostolic tradition was being formed.

Example 1: Early Manuscript Writing and Context

During the second and third centuries, there was no official canon (church-authorized scripture). Many scribes claimed that their manuscripts were authored by the apostles. At that time, controversies centered on Christ being fully human and divine. To protect this duality of the nature of Jesus, scribes altered the understanding of some texts. Biblical scholars commonly accept St. Mark's rendering of the voice of heaven's pronouncement at Jesus's baptism in the Jordan River as an example of a probable alteration of the early manuscripts.[22] "This day I have begotten you, you are the Son of God," is understood by many scholars to be the original text, and this text has been modified to "You are my beloved Son in whom I am well pleased" (Mark 1:11). Why has this happened? Researchers are confident that scribes made changes to dispel any doubts about the divine nature of the Son of God from His incarnation onward, since Jesus could not have become divine (empowered) at His baptism. St. Jerome inserted the words "voice from heaven" (Isaiah 40:4) to authenticate the Son of God as the Messiah, as he wrote the Latin Vulgate (common) translation. I suspect both texts have a source in the Old Testament, and these texts have been applied to Jesus as proof that He is the Messiah. We may never know if the original use of the "Son of God" in the New Testament was any different from its use in the Old Testament.

By the fourth century, we have a statement set in stone. The understanding here could be interpreted as truly different. There appears to be less emphasis placed on the power of baptism, which, not figuratively but actually, made the new believers sons and daughters of God, as Jesus was affirmed to be.[23] Originally, the nature of the incarnation was not a focal point so much as a believer becoming the son or daughter of God when accepting

Jesus and the good news from the Father.[24] There is strength to the claim that, at Jesus's baptism, the words of God's voice were altered to protect the divine and human nature of Jesus from any heretical misunderstanding. At the time of His conception, Jesus was God. There was no other way to consider the Son of God.

Of course, we can only suppose what would have happened to the theology of the incarnation if we find that early in history, Jesus was not thought to have arrived fixed and ready to do His Father's will. St. Luke's comment (Luke 2:52) about Jesus growing in wisdom, stature, and favor with God and men could have been the focus of more heated discussions even into our time. The point of this change in the text was for early Christians to see that the Son of God (Jesus) was the fulfillment of the Jewish understanding about being the son of God (of whom there were many in the Old Testament). The scholars insist we should have the special voice saying, "I have begotten you." This last statement changes the understanding of what it means to be the Son of God from the time of the incarnation, as opposed to receiving that title when He was baptized. The point of this discussion is not so much to take sides in the controversy as to understand that, under external pressures, there has been an evolution of belief taking place.

Example 2: St. Luke and the Humanity of Jesus

In St. Luke's gospel and his Acts of the Apostles, Jesus suffered and died, leading the believer to experience guilt, repentance, and finally salvation.[25] Redemption (salvation) comes after repentance. The early disciples preached this ordered approach to redemption. Nowhere else in Luke's gospel, except in chapter 22, does he say that the death of Jesus alone was itself redemption—not guilt, repentance, and then redemption. The apostles did not preach Jesus's death as redemption for sin, yet Mark 14:22 and Luke

22:19 both say Jesus's death is "for you." This occurs when Luke has Jesus saying, "My body which is *for you* ... my blood poured out *for you*" (italics added). This would be like saying His body and blood are given for you because you need redemption. Besides this anomaly, Jesus's immediate declaration about His body and blood in this narrative presents a disconnection. For instance, it would be like saying, "This is why we are talking about it—that is, Jesus's death as redemption: because Jesus was of real body and real blood."[26] The two statements represent two different ideas that are not connected. Luke and Mark preached that the death of Jesus brings redemption, but His death itself is not redemption. Redemption comes after guilt and repentance. Early disciples preached the same way in the Acts and did not center on the flesh of Jesus as being real flesh and the blood as being real blood. Many scholars believe this statement about Jesus's flesh and blood being connected directly with redemption was added to make it clear to heretics that Jesus was truly human, did suffer, did bleed, and finally died.

In the pursuit of a defense against the heretics, the early Christians were not concerned about redemption (atonement) so much as that Jesus was truly human in flesh and blood. The reader may be somewhat confused by this explanation, but the purpose of this example is to show that the original manuscripts were altered somewhat in favor of the urgent need to defend against any belief that Jesus was not human. The evolution of belief has taken another turn.

In addition to the atonement, the question is, did Christ mean His flesh and blood, or was His "final supper" to be a memorial meal? The latter is more credible. Luke has inserted two Passover meals in chapter 22. The first narrative is more of a commemorative meal, where Luke has Jesus saying that this is the last meal until the kingdom comes. I believe this narrative to be the authentic last supper, the reason being there were not yet controversies about Jesus being truly human. The second "last supper" narrative (Luke 22:19–20) is thought by most textual critics to be a postresurrection narrative and represents the early Christian community's sacred and memorial meal shared with one another. As one would expect, this second "last supper" meal does mention redemption ("poured out for you"). Jesus's real body and blood now become the focal point. The revelation that verses 19 and 20 are additions and intentional in nature had serious consequences for the way the theology of the Eucharist works itself out in the following centuries. At any rate, this consideration leaves one wondering if this single addition (and some similar ones in the other gospels and Acts) may have turned Christian thought and worship in a new direction.

Example 3: St. Paul and Women in the Church

Lastly, an interesting item on the textual criticism list is the statement that St. Paul makes in his first letter to Timothy 2:11–15: "Let a woman learn in silence with full submission." This passage is a statement about the value of women in the assembly, and it contradicts how Paul extols Junia in Romans 16:7, where he appreciates this woman as a "foremost apostle." In 1 Corinthians 14:34, what is of note is how this passage was intentionally added without any effort at continuity.

> Verse 33: Prophets can always control their prophetic spirits, since God is not a God of disorder but of peace.
>
> Verse 34: As in all the churches of the saints, women are to remain quiet at meetings since they

have no permission to speak; they must keep in the background as the Law itself lays it down. If they have any questions to ask, they should ask their husbands at home; it does not seem right for a woman to raise her voice at meetings.

Verse 35: Do you think the word of God came out of yourselves? Or that it has come only to you? Anyone who claims to be a prophet or inspired ought to recognize that what I am writing to you is a command from the Lord.

If one omitted the passage on women (verse 34), the whole discourse would be smooth and integrated. Latest research indicates this to be the case, as a scribe's alteration mark was discovered on an ancient manuscript. The early Christian community placed women in a minor role as the germinal form of the early hierarchy evolved. Admittedly, this was the cultural custom in many of the communities in the Middle East. Unfortunately, this stance regarding women became firm and accepted in the Catholic Church and lasts to this day, inasmuch as sacramental and leadership roles are presently male-dominated.

Nearly all modern scriptural theologians agree that scribes altered numerous passages as the Holy Bible became more accepted and preached throughout the world. Admittedly, scholars claim the vast majority of alterations and deletions appear as accidental and minor, taking into account that scribes abbreviated many words in the early manuscripts.[27] Misinterpretation of abbreviations became rampant among the unprofessional scribes in Palestine and northern Africa. I believe the whole idea of divine inspiration of the written word should have been reevaluated many centuries ago. Jesus taught, for the most part, in parable form, and this form of teaching was culturally restrictive. Still, we know His good news (the Word) made a triumphant entry into every century of the Christian community's story. Scholars have lost some of the intent of these stories, but the overall picture of Jesus is still visible, and indeed, in one sense, we can say that the Word is still divine and eternal.

We have discussed examples of how textual criticism plays a vital role in a more scientific analysis of the written word. Scholars preserved and modified passages they thought to be core doctrines or practices in a rapidly growing church community. A common objection to the purpose of textual criticism arises from the concept of revelation, especially in the Catholic Church. There are two sources of revelation in the Catholic Church. They are Holy Scripture and apostolic tradition (broadened to include the early fathers of the church). At this time in our discussion on textual criticism, it would be rather pointless to contradict church tradition regarding what has come forward from early Christianity into modern times. However, it would be constructive to illustrate the credibility of textual criticism and its response to apparent challenges found in sacred manuscripts. It now becomes reasonable to broaden the concept of divine inspiration to include the redactions, insertions, and other types of alterations to both the written word of scripture and the teachings of the early fathers. In other words, the early community made changes to preserve those beliefs needed to hold together the deposit of faith at the time. In order to move forward in our own beliefs today, I suggest we accept what happened as an example of the evolution of belief.

Two Resolutions

Two possible resolutions or suggestions to the challenges that textual criticism brings to traditional beliefs are worthy of note.

First, rather than dismiss what happened to manuscripts, let us gather the insights of textual criticism and move ahead with what such endeavors offer, creating a credible sense of belief for modern times. We maintain certain perennial beliefs such as the humanity and divinity of Christ, the concepts of flesh and blood as they become formalized in the Eucharist, and the concept of divine inspiration of the Holy Scriptures. Take these ancient traditional beliefs and accept them for what they were at the time, understanding that they were important at the time, and use them as they are pertinent to us for enhancing our own personal faith experiences. If they do not enhance our faith experiences, put them aside and let them stand the test of time. It will do no good at all, when religious beliefs are at a critical crossroad of relevance in the first place, to shovel, as it were, the whole contents of the store into the dumpster in the back alley.

We need to take what Holy Scripture and Christian tradition have to offer and, using the valuable concepts, move on in our faith. In the future, the science of manuscript criticism, whether it is textual, literary, or historical, will definitely prevail because it is evidence based, but it will not provide the needed and comforting insights for daily living in an already believing community. The science of criticism of texts offers valuable insight about what more than likely happened in the evolution of belief in the early church, but it does not provide the elements of the faith experience when encountering God in our lives at this time. What I am saying with regard to this first viable resolution is that we understand some traditional faith matters only as food for a banquet at which fewer and fewer people are feasting. At the time of St. Thomas Aquinas, philosophers and theologians would entertain themselves with debates about how many angels could stand on the head of a pin. Few attend such a debate in modern times.

The second resolution is to disallow discussions starting with the premise that we cannot challenge doctrines and dogmas. Revelation and inspiration are part of a religious evolutionary process in discovering God. It is important to remember that revelation is the *what* that embodies Christian belief. Inspiration is *how* our items of belief are being transmitted to the Christian (this process is going on even to this day). Never allow any discussion to assume that revelation is set in stone and finished. Always question anyone's insistence that a particular religion owns the copyright to revelation, or how a specific revelation has taken place.

At the beginning of this chapter, I spent some time describing how the movie *Lost in Translation* could have different meanings for different people. Like most works of art, such a quality can be considered a sign of a successfully created work of art. I hope that this discussion on questioning the veracity and truth in biblical manuscripts leaves even more questions and generates more ideas about the artwork involved in the evolution of Christian belief.

6

Conscience Formation in Modern Times

From childhood, our actions have been under the control of some kind of enforceable set of laws. Our parents, teachers, church communities, and other sources were generally both the transmitters and enforcers of that law. We gradually came to call the internalization of those external laws *conscience*. Initially, we could not spell out what it was that urged us to act in a consistent way. Eventually, our minds internalized the norms and led us to the formation of conscience.

This chapter will begin with the common understanding of conscience, treat matters relating to the origin of moral or ethical laws, and finally clarify how the advances of science and technology can affect a Christian's moral decision-making process. The overall intent is to show how Christian teachings must adapt to what is happening in modern times. Our traditional moral beliefs are like baggage that needs constant examination for relevance in today's world. Without slipping into a form of ethical relativism, we can decide a course of action and continue to retain our treasured moral beliefs. Opportunities brought forward by scientific research appear to exist outside and different from the norms set down by traditional Christian moral principles. In order to form a future Christian perspective on conscience, we will have to face these challenges now and even more so in the years to come.

The Nature of Conscience

We can start by defining *conscience*. Conscience is the faculty and/or activity of the intellect by which we make distinctions between right and wrong in our conduct; a moral discrimination; an ethical judgment or sensitivity. In other words, conscience is our conception of right or wrong.[28] Just as an individual is capable of gathering together patterns occurring in nature into his or her mind, calling them principles or laws, so also that person has the ability to abstract and place value on actions in the same way. This type of conviction has to do with what is good for the individual and his or her relationship to other human beings. An individual with a developed and educated conscience is sensitive to what is the best (good) way to act. We can say that a developed conscience operates at levels required for groups of society to persist and live in peace. For purposes of survival, society recognizes patterns of expected behavior as rules we are to follow. Admittedly, there are those who do not have a developed conscience and pursue self-satisfaction at the expense of others. Perhaps such a person simply ignores conscience. Either way, in a morally healthy clan, tribe, or society, this attitude will not be tolerated indefinitely.

Origin of Moral Laws

We have been obeying certain rules of behavior for thousands of years. Moral behavior probably predates most sophisticated religious ordinances by thousands of years. In ancient history (eighteenth century BCE), the code of Hammurabi legislated an "eye for an eye and a tooth for a tooth" policy that, for many centuries, seemed to be successful. The ancient truism "Do unto others as you would have them do unto you" found in the Bible (Matthew 7:12) is probably much older than the Judaic law, formalized after the reorganization of the Jewish state from the period of Babylonian captivity. However, "Love your God with your whole heart, your whole mind, and your whole soul, and love your neighbor as you love yourself" (Matthew 22:37) carries obvious tones of an already organized religious institution. Examples would be the Decalogue and volumes of Hebrew laws (Talmudic literature). Predating any major development in science and technology, these religious laws prescribed how people were to act while, at the same time, purveying an accompanying religious belief with all its pronouncements. Society had punishments in place to keep people in line, and when violations occurred, penalties were meted out in the forms of prison, torture, and in many cases, death.

Since history began, most moral edicts were associated with a religious belief, and were prescriptive[29]—that is, the injunctions had their source in an authority. To question the law was to question the authority behind the law. In early Christian tradition, it was adequate to impose obligations of conscience upon all by virtue of a revelation to a biblical authority figure. Mosaic law played a dominant role, and its interpreters enforced such laws with a supposed equity. With the influence of Hellenistic (Greek) thought upon the developing church, natural law became an accompanying reason behind authoritative statements.[30] Natural law issued from a belief that all of nature exhibited a natural order of things and was binding on a conscience. God ordered such compliance because all creatures must follow the natural order of things. Natural law needed no scrutiny or demonstrable process, since it originated in God.

Christian moral philosophers and theologians also examined matters of conscience from the position and support of Holy Scripture and natural law. To question or to disobey certain ethical guidelines set down in scripture was to sin against not only nature, but also God himself. To this day, the Catholic Church still issues proclamations that its statements originate from scripture, and the understanding of the early fathers of the church. For over seventeen centuries, the church claimed eminent domain over any proclamations relating natural law to God. Therefore, not only must all moral proclamations issued by the church be correct, but the church is the *only* dispenser of the norms of morality as well. The church, being the body of Christ, is the only institution privy to divine revelation of any kind. The church now has a divine authority and is always correct when treating moral matters. Pronouncements on natural law come ultimately from God when properly interpreted by the holy church. The problem here is that, outside an institutional church, few philosophers today accept the concept of a universal natural law that includes an obligatory connotation. Science, with its heavy emphasis on verifiability for the formulation of a law, utilizes descriptive[31] (demonstrable) laws of nature, which carry no obligatory connotation. It is at this point that matters of conscience for the modern Christian hit a wall of uncertainty and confusion.

For over two thousand years, the Judeo-Christian system of ethics has had a lasting influence on matters relating to the education of one's conscience. This system has permeated Western society to its core, supporting, in almost all cases, the enrichment and high standard of life brought on by democratic governments. No one will deny this ethic to be healthy and assuring for most believers. The moral edicts found in Holy Scripture were, for the most part, positive influences. The only exceptions are some laws entrenched in cultural traditions. Even these evolved alongside a more modernized and realistic view of moral conduct and consequent punishment for immoral conduct. Without even a second glance at some ancient laws, our understanding today is noticeably different. We do have laws against adultery, but stoning to death is not a punishment commensurate with the crime. The church admits such, and for the most part, it comes down to how we interpret laws today. Even the church picks and chooses from the Bible what are truly laws or just bad cultural practices.

Challenges that Science and Technology Bring to Decision-Making

Having understood the Christian church's domain over moral codes and education of the conscience of its followers, we need to ask some serious questions. Can technological advances today be subject to moral premises based on the natural order of things and Holy Scripture? Can the interpreters of God's revelation in biblical texts have credible answers and give good direction? Should today's Christian look elsewhere to solve matters relating to conscience? These are questions to which I will offer no answer, only a direction: a direction to put aside outdated notions of natural law and go back to the words and teachings of Jesus, since this is (or should be) the ultimate foundation of the Christian conscience. Jesus summed up His teachings for us in these words: "Love the Lord with all your heart, and your neighbor as yourself ... in this is contained the law and the prophets." If we go back to the basics, the words and teachings of Jesus, we will be more informed (educated), and we can answer these questions ourselves because our responses will ultimately form a catalyst for proper decision-making in the future.

In Vitro Fertilization

As an example, let us look at the topic of in vitro fertilization, presently used to achieve pregnancies for couples unable to conceive.

This medical procedure involves fertilization of an egg outside the female reproductive system. What does the Catholic Church have to say about this new technology?

> Pope Benedict XVI, speaking to members of the Pontifical Academy for life ... warned against "the lure of the technology of artificial insemination," which is not permitted by Catholic teaching ... Catholic teaching prohibits in vitro fertilization, maintaining that a child has a right to be conceived in the marital embrace of his or her parents. Human sexuality has two components, the unitive and procreative; IVF separates these components and makes the procreative its only goal. Pope Paul VI said that there is an "inseparable connection, willed by God, and unable to be broken by man on his own initiative, between the meanings of the conjugal act: the unitive meaning and the procreative meaning."

> There are other issues involved. IVF makes the child a commodity produced in a laboratory, and makes doctors, technicians, and even businesspeople part of the conception process. The sperm used is usually obtained by masturbation, which the church teaches is immoral. The sperm or eggs used may not come from the couple desiring the child; because one of the spouses may be infertile, it may be necessary to use the sperm or eggs from an outsider ... [32]

We may ask numerous questions when reading this portion of the article:

- Where is the church source for the assertion that artificial insemination is immoral?
- What rights does an unconceived child have, and where are these rights enshrined and validated?
- How accurately can any religion define the extent of sexuality?
- How can natural law, created by God, be willed?
- Who has ultimate authority over a couple's conjugal act?
- Where in the Bible is there actual reference to masturbation? (This is discussed in a later chapter.)
- Besides an individual or couple, who has authority over sperm and eggs?

A more enlightening approach might be to evaluate IVF, not from the context of convoluted church teachings and natural law, but from the point of view of Jesus's teachings. A conscience grounded in the teachings of Jesus may instead ask questions like these:

- Does IVF contradict the injunction to love God, our neighbor, or ourselves?
- Can IVF be a source of good?
- Are there circumstances in which it can be a source of harm?

Such questions outline some of the factors that may enter into a proper decision. It is now the responsibility of the Christian to make an educated decision as to the proper course of action to take. By returning to fundamental Christian principles, it is truly possible to educate one's mind, evaluate the relevance of traditional statements, and then, following one's conscience, make a good moral decision about the matter. This is important because in vitro fertilization procedures will continue for some time to come.

Vaccination

It would be helpful to observe how Christian denominations incorporate the use of vaccines into their ethical guidelines for decision making for their members. Some ultra-conservative protestant denominations are quick to denounce such practices for their members, while denominations that are more liberal show approval, with certain restrictions. The Catholic Church, for almost two centuries, has approved of vaccinations. In all instances, the Vatican approves of the use of vaccines for protection of populations vulnerable to diseases that are epidemic in nature. However, the church issues a qualified approval when it comes to vaccines manufactured in part from cells taken from aborted fetuses. I will quote the following article by Rev. Kevin McGovern, director of a center for health ethics in Melbourne, Australia:

> The Catholic Church does not dismiss the problem of ethically compromised vaccines. To the contrary, it calls for research and development of alternative, ethically acceptable vaccines. It also exhorts all people including parents to join in this call. However, until alternative vaccines are developed, it also accepts the use of even these ethically compromised vaccines in order to protect children, pregnant women, and the population as a whole from the risk of contracting serious disease. The teaching of the Catholic Church provides no support of the refusal of vaccination against

serious disease, even if the available vaccines are ethically compromised.[33]

At first glance, one could praise the church for its wise yet qualified approval of the use of ethically compromised vaccines. This would be a good thing to do. However, if one looks closer at the actions of the church in this regard, one would detect a pragmatic approach behind the proclamation. There is a decision made that views the common good over the immorality of abortion. I am not criticizing the church's present position on abortion. I am looking at how the church is adapting itself to the challenge brought on by science and technology.

Even though abortion is taboo in most Christian denominations, in particular the Catholic Church, the overall concern in the vaccination issue is about what is best for the greater good. I am not berating a form of pragmatism (outcome based) at this point. We all exhibit a pragmatic approach to resolving issues in this fast-moving world. Many institutions and governments choose an outcome-based approach at times, rather than acting in accordance with certain values (principle based). What is happening, in most instances, is that people are making decisions based within the context of time, technology, and culture. Two thousand years ago, people never had to make these kinds of decisions. To make present-day moral decisions based solely on support from biblical sources or from interpreters of scriptures (time restrictive) would be highly imprudent. Once again, I hearken back to the old truism, dating back before any religious institution existed and reiterated in the words and teachings of Jesus: do unto others as you would have them do unto you.

I am convinced that an educated conscience is quite capable of making the best decision when faced with personal problems and challenges. Deep within the framework of all living organisms is the drive to preserve life and to propagate a species. This innate drive occurs not just on the individual level, but at community and national levels as well.

This chapter discussed the nature of conscience, the origin of moral laws, and the basis of good decisions in our time. Although quite brief in its content, the chapter's intent was to show how moral statements and decisions are time restrictive, and somewhat culture based. Christian pronouncements in the past have had a dominant influence on our consciences and moral actions. The examples cited indicate a change in position for the church as it struggles to adapt to the advances in science and technology. The problem with a biblical source as the key instructor in ethics is that moral questions are much more sophisticated and difficult to solve today. Interpreters of Holy Scripture and the teachings of the early fathers of the church fall short of being adequate guides for our moral decision-making. I did not give answers to resolve specific challenges. However, the universal truth and golden rule about doing unto others as you would have them do unto you is a partial answer and gives us at least a direction.

7

The Power of Good and Evil

The intent of this chapter is to inform the reader how and why we use religion to explain bad behavior, the unfortunate natural disasters occurring in our world, and illnesses described as demon-possession. We will delve into the history of how spirits became the purveyors of good and evil. Second, I will discuss why someone as infinitely good and compassionate as God and His beloved Son could allow such evil, pain, and suffering in the world. We have difficulty understanding how God, respecting humans' free will, allows Satan to wreak havoc in our world. On the one hand, we enjoy all the good things God has given us, and yet, He has allowed millions of people to die needlessly and suffer incredible pain with death-dealing diseases, such as cancer. Why do we think this way? It is an issue which, at first glance, appears irresolvable. Lastly, I have included a brief discussion on the nature of free will and how it relates to doing good and avoiding evil. What I have to share in this chapter will undoubtedly be difficult for some to accept, but hopefully it will provide for others an insightful and reasonable explanation of such responses as "The devil made me do it" and "God's ways are not our ways."

One of the most difficult tasks is to understand the concept of good and evil. From childhood, a parental technique to get the desired results in the educational process was to levy the huge sanction of a deity's revenge and punishment for an evil or immoral action. This technique probably predates biblical history. However, psychology teaches us there is good reason to question the effectiveness of any kind of threat. In the short term, it brings a measure of temporary relief. All Christians have been educated in the moral imperative of doing good and avoiding evil. One way of insuring good actions is a warning that God is watching and judging our actions. For adults and children alike, our moral lives become quite complex when the devil or Satan enters into the mix. Let us look at the evolution of belief on the matter.

Ancient Spirits

In ancient Mesopotamian myth, the origin of evil comes from an amorphous eternal entity called chaos. We have discussed this entity earlier in our treatment of creation. Chaos within Mesopotamian myth brought on not only confusion in creation, but evil as well. The personification of evil took place many centuries later, as Jewish literature contained personifications such as Satan and his cohorts of fallen angels.[34] Remember that most religions practiced polytheism at the time of the early Hebrew culture. Jewish ancestors may even have entertained practices to the lesser gods.[35]

While in captivity, the Israelites were attempting to preserve and develop a sense of their ancestral monotheistic belief in the face of ancient pagan influence. Reference to Satan occurs more than thirty times in the New Testament. In Matthew's gospel, the evangelist has Jesus witnessing the fall of Lucifer.[36] The acceptance of the evil one was set and in place by the fourth century CE, as Christians believed Satan to be an angel who had rebelled against God.[37] We are told that God created Satan, who, when he appears in our world, tempts and torments us. To maintain that Satan is created indicates a spiritual being having the ability to take on material qualities. Such a belief was common among the ancients and would be a concept similar to the demigods (half god, half human) who are found in Greek mythology.

From the traditional beliefs of the ancients, we have created a being (Satan) and personified him as a spiritual being who enters into our space and time. Such a premise is unsupportable, even though the gospel relates instances where Jesus was casting demons from people and animals. If one follows the logic behind the belief in the personification of evil, then such beliefs fall into the domain of the physical and, as such, must be verifiable in some way. However, they are not demonstrable by physical evidence and eventually will not stand the test of time. As we look back into ancient history, we notice good spirits and evil demons playing a dominant role in a community's life. Is there some value to ascribing to God the responsibility for both good and unfortunate happenings? It is possible, but such a belief is becoming more and more questionable.

Blaming a Deity: the Easy Way Out

Why does a supreme being matter to the physical world? The reason why a supreme being matters is that people cannot tolerate random consequences and happenings in their lives. What makes humans different from other animals is that we are continually looking for the meaning behind everything. There always has to be a reason why good and bad things happen to us. We think there is bad and evil in nature and fail to realize that nature is neither bad nor good. Nature simply *is,* and it is not controlled by a deity. However, a common explanation for a natural catastrophe, evil, pain, suffering, and death is that our creator is behind it, or at least permits such things to happen. God is the reason why un-explainable things happen to us. The more primitive the religious practice, the more likely this kind of belief prevails. To explain some of the evil in our world, we personify it and its source.

The presence of God was so entrenched in religious belief that it was thought that God actually resided in certain locales. In places sacred to the Hebrews, we have the Ark of the Covenant and the temple as God's house, not just places of prayer. In ancient times, God's house was carried into battle. If a battle was lost, God willed it because the Israelites had disobeyed an order from on high. When we run up against the intersection of ourselves with personal death-dealing events, we bring God into the scenario as well. We continue to petition God and pray that God see things our way. Why is this? The answer lies in the need to make our own interests the focal point and to make God's interests our own. This is, in essence, a form of manipulation. Furthermore, any type of public or private devotional experience perpetuating this motive only exacerbates the problem, and with this thinking, a satisfactory resolution will never occur. We cannot blame God for things happening, nor can we attempt to control Him with petitions and promises.

The nature of prayer and meditation is not a focal point for this work. However, it is very helpful to communicate with God as a power arising from within. When it appears that the world is turning upside down, the achievement of "mindfulness" provides amazing positive benefits for well-being and peace. Several eastern religions have perfected this form of prayer and oftentimes call it meditation. The power of the kingdom of God comes from within, and a good prayer life is the best way to tap into the healing power of the presence of God. Prayer and meditation can help us rid ourselves of the many "demons" we face in our lives.

The Devil Did Not Make Me Do It

Temptation plays an important role in the traditional moral teaching among Christians. A major step in the pedagogical approach to sin is in the preventative measures taken upon the occasion of sin (temptation), as well as the sin itself. The attempt is understandable, in that strengthening the power of free will to do the right thing usually produces a positive effect. However, it is not good pedagogy to associate the source of the temptation with an external evil force like Satan and his cohorts. There is no personification of the source of evil that is going to strengthen the will to do good and avoid evil. In fact, to live with the devil on your back may very well result in the opposite effect. Attributing wrongdoing to an external entity can result in blaming something or someone else for our own shortcomings.

It is beneficial to see how scriptural theologians have viewed the concept of temptation. In most passages in the Old Testament, we find God putting the chosen ones to a test of some sort, by a warning, by enticement, or by bringing on a form of suffering. In later Jewish manuscripts, the writer personifies this form of temptation, as in the book of Job.[38] In this instance, the intent is to elicit a faith declaration and sincerity from Job. In the New Testament, Jesus's prayer (the "Our Father") refers to a form of deliverance from something that humankind is capable of overcoming. Almost all modern interpreters of Jesus's temptation in the desert ascribe a doctrinal symbolism to this episode rather than an accurate description of an actual event.[39] One thing is for certain: there was no drone taking in every word and action that occurred on the mountaintop or in the desert. The temptation of Jesus by Satan is probably more of an expansion of what salvation, bread, and power meant for the Christians during the early days of persecution.[40]

The personification of evil has produced rituals and other activities that are unacceptable in modern society. Liturgists need to abolish these rituals with all their trappings. Rituals like blessing things and people with holy water are about as close to an attempt to manipulate God or the devil as one can get. In another chapter, I will treat the topic of religious rituals and ceremonies as being both valuable and questionable events in a believer's life of faith. Any religious activity or belief that passes on the responsibility for bad action to the devil is not valuable or productive. Such activity will not stand the test of time for the modern believer. It becomes less credible and more unsatisfactory to attribute evil to an external entity as the cause of our own shortcomings in the commission of an evil act.

Exorcism

When researching the history of exorcism, the scholar will find that two observations always surface. The first observation is that the more ancient and primitive a society, the more superstitious and prevalent the beliefs and cultural practices are for that given group of people. These beliefs and practices involve the casting out of demons, the curing of incurable afflictions caused by powerful spiritual entities, and, finally, the dissolution of curses placed upon certain individuals and groups. The second observation, which we can trace into modern times, is the dominance of a powerful individual (exorcist) or institution over a rather ignorant, fearful, and dependent people. The more remote and isolated groups, clans, and tribes are today, the more such practices occur.

The casting out of spirits is rare in the Old Testament. In the book of Tobit, a supposed angel (Gabriel?) is involved. However, in most cases, it was God casting out demons and crushing the enemies of Israel. All evil came about by not following the dictates of the God of Israel. In the New Testament, it was common to cast out demons. Christ cast out demons. The interesting point here is that we can correlate such actions with what the writers of the gospel called healing and its spiritual component, the forgiveness of sins. Afflictions were associated with some kind of sinfulness of the individual or the person's ancestry. Most cures performed by Christ and His disciples, as well as others, were associated with forgiveness of sins. The few that do not involve forgiveness would, in my mind, be later insertions into the text and somewhat questionable.

The use of the term *exorcism* begins to appear in the third century and was directly referred to by St. Cyril (circa 355 CE) in relation to acts or precise words during ceremonial baptisms. We call these functions *minor exorcisms*, and the clergy exercised these special powers as early as 236–250 CE under the leadership of Pope Fabian.[41] Ministers still perform minor exorcisms during baptism of catechumens even to this day. The intent of such prayers is to ask God's assistance for protection from Satan and his power, as well as protection from temptation. The format of these rituals resides outside the interest and the domain of science. Scientists do not know all the physiological, hormonal, and biochemical influences upon the brain, and few demonstrable conclusions surface. Much has yet to be learned about alterations in brain function due to drugs and cerebral injuries as well. I will treat healing and the placebo effect in a later chapter.

The common person's understanding of exorcism today involves a violent scenario, oftentimes accompanied by a form of punishment. Stories of violent exorcisms are rampant in the media because of the influence of the motion picture and other video industries. Expectations are that, with the dawn of science and education of the masses, there would be fewer such instances surfacing, but far from it. Many are attracted by the theater of the bizarre, and the more horrific and bloody the scenario, the more popular the story.

Pope Benedict XVI was somewhat cautious with regard to exorcism. However, Pope Francis has openly promoted the work of exorcists and has, in the past, commissioned nearly a hundred priests to perform these special exorcisms.[42] It is unfortunate that the Catholic Church still holds on to the vestigial remains of an ancient practice instead of using appropriate sources for clarifying and diminishing ignorance and superstition. In such cases, violent or otherwise, it would be much better to call 911 for the police and ambulance. Doctors of psychology and psychiatry would be the best resource.

Free Will or Not

For over the last two centuries, Christians have been listening to the ongoing debates on whether humans truly possess a free will. Discussions about free will seem to be invariably connected to doing good and avoiding evil. This is so because we are at the center of acts that we call sinful acts. I think we need to talk about free will because free will is most often associated with personal acts of good and evil. However, some philosophers today maintain that we are determined to act in a certain way from the time of conception in our mothers' wombs. The following represents a brief summary of their arguments.

1. Laws of the universe determine us in every aspect of our existence.

2. The type of genetics in our bodies could predict the way we act.

3. The idea that we are or can be responsible for our actions because of a free will is a figment of our imagination.

4. We act in a certain way because our minds have been fashioned to follow a course of action predetermined by a set of needs and wants.

This type of thinking is an attempt to reduce our responsibility for doing good and avoiding evil. Given restrictions on the ability to choose to do something, are we truly free? It is my belief that we do have a free will, although with qualifications. We may think we have a free will, but our free will is not altogether free in every sense of the term.

When describing a type of behavior as being good or bad, we are actually defining it according to a designated moral code set in place for the common good. We declare good behavior as important for the greater good of society, as well as for the greater good of a smaller community, such as family. The type of behavior known as moral behavior is both determined and free at the same time. Some aspects of behavior are innate and determined, while other aspects are not determined. This is why I mentioned earlier that we do have free will but one that is not altogether free. At times, our innate drive to preserve an aspect of our lives can generate an act that seems to be a violation of a moral code. It is not possible within this work to elaborate in detail on all the ramifications of a free will being partially determined. There are many judicial court systems that have tediously mapped out how this is indeed the case, and the seriousness of the guilt oftentimes hangs on the limitations of free will with regard to an act.

Further consideration about the existence of free will relates to research psychology involving willpower and self-control. Recent studies by Roy Baumeister at Florida State University indicate that the less glucose present in the brain, the less self-control present.[43] The portion of the intellectual area of the brain that controls free will is biochemically dependent on glucose for proper functioning. The mind does not perform independent of the brain. What this means is that willpower and self-control (also known as free will) are body dependent. This function of the brain is what sets us apart from other species, in that the willpower is the engine that directs us into a healthier and safer future. Nature has given us this unique function, even though it comes with a variety of constraints.

Relating Free Will to Religious Precepts

As the content of Christian precepts evolves in modern times, we should be aware of some cautionary pitfalls. First, be very careful of specific dictates in the Old and New Testaments. Hold on to the general moral statements made for society at large, and treat as less valuable any moral statements encased within the lifestyle of a community's history. Religious and moral beliefs continue to evolve and are, in many instances, restricted by the context and interpretation of a given time. Secondly, it is important to note that accountability for one's actions is validly placed when one freely chooses to perform an act that is in itself moral or immoral. Doing evil to one's neighbor cannot and will never be justified by a complaint that the neighbor was unjust to one in the past. Lastly, attitudes and actions that display similarities to parental or a previous community's conditions are no reason to perpetuate immoral and decadent lifestyles. Two wrongs never make a right. On the other hand, being good to one's neighbor, in most situations, generates not hatred and evil but fulfillment and happiness.

As Christianity evolves in its understanding of good and evil, there will always be pressures on the Christian believer arising from societal mores that tend to soften the seriousness of responsibility for one's actions. Oftentimes groups outwardly refuse to shoulder the responsibility for their actions. However, in general, we should follow the basic message promoted by Christ, such as doing good to others as you would have them do unto you. By doing this, the Christian expresses and gives witness to the basic values of preserving life, in all its aspects and within each community, even as societal networks grow more complex in the global community.

The phenomenon of doing good and avoiding evil is part of the educated human condition. It is my belief that there will always be some kind of a general moral code built into a society. We define what is good and evil with a system of ethics. Aspects of any ethical system will always continue to indicate alterations and adaptations, but a basic belief in being good and just to others will never go away. At the same time, while many may not be aware of it, when the genuine and sincere Christians perform good actions, they are truly conquering the force of evil brought on by bad people—and not by a God that allows evil things to happen.

8

Science, a Potential Ally for Purifying Christian Belief

This chapter will attempt to examine some religious dictates that require oversight and reworking for satisfying a questioning mind. It is my belief that science is and could be a welcome ally in purifying belief systems. A Christian can do this by sifting out erroneous injunctions from the past. It is imperative that a Christian always evaluate any legislation that a religious institution proclaims. Using selected topics, I intend to show how science can become a true ally in evaluating church laws and other legislation rooted in Christian tradition.

Decision-Making and the Informed Conscience

One of the most challenging endeavors for a Christian believer is to persevere through an attitude of apathy. Why should we pursue a deeper belief and acceptance of Christian traditions? Our knowledge of the real world outstrips and possibly discredits some values gained from present-day religious practices. It is true that Holy Scripture and Jesus's parables, passed on for our faith and prayer, do have perennial value. However, is there any more value to myth than as an adolescent religious educational tool? I am convinced there really is a deep value to accepting much that tradition has passed on, as long as there is oversight present to control any prescriptive obligatory statements attached to the reality of these myths.

The church constantly issues statements on morality and immorality, doing so under the title of an unquestionable authority. In the past, to adamantly disagree and not follow religious directions resulted in excommunication, punishment, or spiritual banishment of some kind. In the eyes of the church, it is the duty of believers to inform themselves of the moral duties of a Christian. If the uninformed conscience does not seek to be informed, at that point the conscience is then an immoral entity, guilty of something. The problems today are apathy and the refusal to face any conflict. We could leave controversial issues for another generation to resolve. I believe that if church authorities do not do something soon, the huge bulldozer of science will catastrophically roll over and discredit any valuable religious beliefs received through Christian tradition.

The Dalai Lama once said that if there are any conflicts between scientific truths and a particular religious tenet or practice, it is the religious belief that must take a back seat, and we must envision new insights from a religious point of view.[44] This means there is an adaptive process evident. Beliefs now have an oversight (scientific data) as a challenger. Science is now in the position of providing oversight when overlapping occurs. It is a refreshing and liberating possibility. Just because the Bible dictates what we ought to do in scenarios such as unwed motherhood, spousal infidelity, polygamy, slavery, and the like, this database could not possibly match up to what we have knowledge of today. Furthermore, science is constantly reloading the database, providing our minds with ever-changing and developing insights. Science helps build an informed foundation of facts that generate better insights into how we should live our Christian lives today.

Whatever one may call this sifting process of science, it must always call into question a blind adherence to any religious belief that overlaps into nature and the world of science. Conversely, science is not a spiritual and moral handbook from which one can derive answers. Rather, science purifies our database and constantly gives us fresh views of what things are and what they could be.

It would be good at this point to clarify my thinking on science and matters related to religious belief. Recall that the intent of this book is to show how Christianity has evolved as external pressures have come to bear on the expression of its religious belief. Necessity and practicality play a significant role with regard to changes in cultures and societies. In the same way, events like the formal schism of the tenth and eleventh centuries, papal corruption in the Middle Ages, the invention of the printing press, the Reformation, and the industrial revolution have had much influence on changes in church law and the understanding of early doctrines and theological thinking. There is no doubt that Christian thought has evolved regarding the traditional doctrines set down by the early fathers. To think otherwise is to bury one's head in the sand. The Galileo controversy is just one example where church tradition has had to back away due to the force of facts and evidence. The way things are will constantly change.

The following topics will be an exposé of what I mean by science and religious belief working together to provide healthy outcomes for religious believers. It is very important that Christians be able to move ahead with an enriched religious experience of Christ without being entrenched in some inadequate ancient traditions, practices, and beliefs. Bear with me as I treat some church teachings (not all), and how science affects these teachings through factual evidence.

Family Planning

If you are a devout Christian and you have no concerns of conscience about the planned size of your family, you are welcome to skip to the next section of this chapter. For the rest of you, this section may offer some direction in determining the proper role of conscience in family planning.

A hundred years ago, the life span of the average person worldwide was fifty years. In the past, the reason for this low life span was due to poor sanitation and infectious diseases. After we simply took steps to control the spread of diseases in the maternity ward, the survival rate of infants mushroomed to unheard-of numbers. The introduction of antibiotics and blood transfusions in the twentieth century resulted in saving millions of young and adult patients.

We certainly live in a different yet, I believe, better world today. Although challenges exist, the potential for living a better life is obvious in countries where people are truly free. The standard of living and health benefits, along with cultural practices, can actually mature and flourish, resulting in life spans unheard of in recorded history. There was a higher birthrate in the last century. One plausible explanation for the higher birthrate in earlier times is that there was no birth control. Another reason is that families just arrived and were not planned. Today, people are much more successful in raising children into adulthood. However, it is possible that the time, energy, and expense of raising two children today is like raising many more children a hundred years ago. Planning the size of a family in today's world is a concern because couples are also getting married later in life. For adults, there are many more things to consider than just raising a family. Technology today is very demanding in terms of education and preparation for a professional career. Mobility in the workforce is now a global affair rather than being limited to a workplace in the next village.

It now makes perfect sense for the educated conscience to move ahead with measures to ensure the proper sizing of a family. In the past, to limit the size of a family was tantamount to a form of forbidden birth control. Many pastors counseled parishioners to be aware of the moral dangers of family planning. In many cases, the priest and minister were biased in their direction for parents. For all practical purposes, priests and ministers felt they had a place in the bedroom of the modern believer. A supposed "natural family planning," espoused by some churches, although still encouraged, falls short in its objective. Such a directive is somewhat unrealistic and demanding regarding abstinence for the duration of ovulation. The informed mind, along with a conscience freed from any guilt, needs to make decisions about how to live a healthy and satisfying family life. Life is different today, and young people do not need to burden themselves with advice taken from ancient and outdated religious traditions. In marital matters, to be open to procreation must take on a different meaning. We need to understand that parents bear the obligation of determining family size and correct parenting. Family planning is a requirement in today's world, and science can be of help, but science does not tell you how this is to take place. Couples may not wish to have any children for a number of valid reasons. No one should be in a position of judging ill of couples, as they have the right to live their lives with consciences at peace. The forward thinking of the Christian on this matter indicates a definite shift in attitude and, before long, will result in a change of thought within the religious institution itself. There are very qualified professional family planners available who can dispel any possible guilt a couple may have about family size. These health counselors can provide good direction for planning family size, especially when personal health challenges are involved.

Contraception

Contraception and birth control may appear to be similar due to the outcome of the restriction of the number of births. There is a correlation, but they are not the same. The intent of contraception is to prevent the union of a sperm and egg, or to prevent the viability of a fertilized egg in the female reproductive system. Contraception is preventive in the sense of controlling birth in a population. This is the extent of its application. Contraception is just one form of birth control. In Christian and Catholic tradition, such an action is immoral because nothing should interfere with a primary purpose of the procreative act. Such a proscription is believed to fall under natural law (thought to be the domain of religion), and no one was allowed to challenge this understanding of natural law.

Some theologians maintain a scriptural basis for declaring any kind of birth control as evil. Even as late at the sixteenth century, a very imaginative biologist maintained that he saw a little human being in a sample of sperm cells.[45] This example, of course, would support the Mosaic law, which prohibits killing another human being.

All the confusion for young married couples comes from outdated and incorrect religious legislation. The church's intrusion into the bedroom has caused endless problems that will never be resolved unless couples break away from the bonds that tie them down to irrational edicts. Once again, it is within the domain of the informed conscience to determine the actions regarding contraception. Doctors do need to play a greater role in this information process. Reasons for condemning contraception have no valid basis in scripture and are dependent on a law that does not line up with any natural order of things as we understand it today.

Abortion

We can define abortion as the active killing in the womb, resulting in the delivery of a dead embryo or fetus. The process results in the termination of a pregnancy, which is the general intent of all the procedures. An initial summary is appropriate. At fertilization, there is the formation of a human genetic code. In pregnancy, we understand that the first eight weeks focus on the developing and positioning of tissues, the embryonic stage. After the second month, with the tissues in place, the fetal stage moves the process through the rest of a nine-month gestation. With modern technology, a woman can detect pregnancy within a matter of days after fertilization of her egg(s). The detection of certain pregnancy hormones allows a woman to make an important decision even prior to event of her next menstrual period. Occasionally there are ectopic and tubal pregnancies, resulting in therapeutic abortions. In performing a therapeutic abortion, the intent of the doctor is to preserve the life of the mother. The Catholic Church and some other Christian churches have condoned such procedures, since the fetus could be considered an "unjust aggressor" and the mother an "innocent victim."[46] Some ethicists will take issue with the use of the words *unjust aggressor*. Nonetheless, such pregnancies, if continued, would result in the death of not only the baby, but the mother as well.

The fifth commandment in Mosaic law says, "You shall not kill," and Christian belief strongly upholds this law. Supporting this injunction is the ancient law of doing unto others as you would have them do unto you. If you maintain that an undeveloped member of the human species is human, then there is no need to pursue this topic further. You are on a firm footing.

We can ask ourselves what it is that fuels the apparent need for thousands of abortions each year on our continent. When analyzing justifications for abortions, we find the most common ones are these: the fetus is not human; it does not have rights as a human; a woman has rights over her own body; or the baby is, in some way, unwanted.

I do not choose at this time to judge the value of any or all of the numerous justifications for having an abortion. However, I would like to illustrate how good decision-making can take place when we look at the big picture of life. Having taught biology all my life, I can say every form of life has a built-in drive to preserve itself. This is not a moral matter or a supposed natural order of things. There is no moral content in this drive. There is no obligatory (good or evil) dimension to this drive. It is just there.

There are exceptions to the "law of preservation of species," but the exceptions do not appear to be focused on an organism's needs and wants. Though rare, abortions do occur in lower animal life. However, the drive to stay alive constitutes what evolution is about. In the course of evolution, species make use of mutations in a population for necessary adaptation purposes for preservation. If the species cannot adapt, it disappears off the radar of biological history.

The final question on this matter is, are our decisions about the unborn in line with the big picture? I imagine in some cases, abortion could be consistent with nature. At our stage in evolutionary history, that stance is not clear in my mind, but, for good reason, possibly in other minds. Think it over. I listed justifications for abortion earlier in this section. Given that the nature of human life is to preserve itself, and given your circumstances, are those reasons for having an abortion good enough to satisfy your conscience? If so, then you should act accordingly. However, remember that there is nothing more important in making ethical decisions than being a decision maker with an educated conscience.

Nature's protest is that life is its mandate. I have discussed with the reader, in brief, what I have found to be the case, regardless of what any institution says. An informed conscience makes a decision based on a reasonable conviction of the mind. Condemn no one, but rather, if able, hold fast to what nature is teaching.

Assisted Death

Doctor-assisted suicide looms on the horizon as a very controversial topic that nations are attempting to resolve in various ways. It is important not to confuse doctor-assisted suicide with the practice of euthanasia, which refers more to the practice of relieving people or animals from unnecessary suffering. The Catholic Church loudly condemns any such procedures for human beings during the final rite of passage. God gave life, and God will choose when an individual leaves this life. For decades, some religious institutions, e.g. the Catholic Church, have maintained that no one needs to take extraordinary means to keep a dying person alive, but also that no one should actively end a person's life. For some time now, the controversy has shifted into the public domain, with governments taking their own particular stance on the matter. There are many such classifications put forward that account for how death may take place. *Assisted suicide, doctor-assisted suicide, medically assisted suicide,* and other terms come forward, depending on how influential a vested interest group may be in a particular country.

In the United States, several jurisdictions presently have some form of assisted suicide in place. What is of note in this controversy is that animals in acute distress were always euthanized to prevent unnecessary pain and suffering, yet humans, even upon consent, were not allowed to have such procedures taken on their behalf. Humans do not always have a "good death." Age, consent due to seriousness of the illness, and proximity to death all make any political decision to enact a law on the matter very complex, difficult, and predictably wrong in many regions of the world. Whatever a governmental pronouncement on the matter might be, uncertainty may exist. Would it still be in the power of the Christian conscience to decide what should take place in a particular instance, when suffering is extreme and death is imminent? It will be some time before a satisfactory answer is given.

Science and technology find themselves on both sides of this political, social, and human issue. It is because of science that people are living to be much older, and this carries with it health problems for the aged in numbers unheard of before this time. Furthermore, appropriate palliative care has resulted in a less painful period in preparation for the passing of a patient. As one prepares for death, interactions with the family and community are extremely valuable and wholesome, and could be a healing experience. We know that we should always give the "will to live" a chance. On the other hand, science has provided doctors and others with appropriate and nonintrusive methods for a humane and quick end to unacceptable suffering due to terminal illnesses or injuries. One could very legitimately ask, what is the point of obvious and horrible pain and suffering? Would I be able to say, if I happened to be the patient, that I choose not to suffer a horrible and drawn-out death?

It is very easy to stand back and make a judgment based on traditional religious beliefs, because such decisions could release one from a sense of guilt. A decision made solely on the religious belief that God gives life and therefore God alone takes life is not adequate for the informed conscience of today. A valid question arises for the modern believer. Why would a doctor provide to animals (all of which have received life from God) a quick end to interminable pain and suffering, but not allow the same to happen, upon consent, to human beings? I believe a doctor of veterinary medicine would never allow an animal to suffer needlessly until it dies a natural death.

It is important to distinguish euthanasia from doctor-assisted suicide. The two are radically different. There is no possible consent available from an animal, but consent from a cogent human being is necessary. The ideal situation would be that all people near death could pass away in a painless peace. Nevertheless, an ideal is exactly what it is, an ideal. An ideal is not always achievable.

With careful monitoring in place, it is highly doubtful that over an extended period the number of doctor-assisted suicides would greatly increase. To choose to live is a decision that we carry in our psychological structure. However, we must remember that, in certain instances, a person could have a clear conscience in choosing the alternative, death, even if some might consider it a lesser evil. We cannot make condemning judgments upon someone's personal choice. Rather, we need to show compassion and put all effort into preserving life, if possible.

Masturbation

Of all controversial subjects treated in this chapter, I find the topic of masturbation most disconcerting. From puberty, I (along with most Catholic teenagers) was instructed that such an act is immoral. Consequences of such an act would result in a mortally sinful condition, and if one died before confessing such an act, hell would certainly be the judgment. This abhorrent type of religious instruction drove a deep black mark of fear in my psyche and in the minds of other Catholic male youths. I was taught that ejaculation was a normal process for teenage boys, but to take pleasure from orgasm was like eating of the forbidden fruit. I was not aware that anyone discussed female sexual pleasure with the same gravity as male gratification. Perhaps young women were the targets of similar severe threats from teaching nuns and may also have been taught that having such pleasure was sinful. However, as young men, we were not aware of anything except the threats from our priest instructors, who happened to be our confessors. Looking back, I realize it was a completely bizarre situation. How is it that the Christian church persists in this form of teaching? Moral theologians, as always, did find justification by interpreting Holy Scripture in obscure ways. However, let us visit some directions given through modern scientific approach.

Laws of nature (derived from the evidence of science) indicate that foreplay (preparing for the act of coitus) occurs in almost all higher forms of mammalian species. As a youth, struggling to work my way through this dark hole, it became very clear in my mind that I needed to discuss with non-Christian youths what they thought the consequences would be for masturbation. Their responses were truly a revelation. In every instance, I was told that parental guidance indicated such acts were natural and that one should not get overly upset when they occurred in the shower or one's bedroom. The young man is simply preparing for adulthood. Advice was given not to be obsessed with the matter—not to worry unless the activity became so frequent that it turned one's social relationship inward, preventing the enrichment of friendships with both young men and women. I sincerely maintain that the church's strict teaching on the matter has not changed an iota, even though the confessional experience may have softened a bit.

The Catholic Church's past teaching on masturbation was based on a strict and inappropriate interpretation of the incident of Onan, a mythic figure in Genesis 38, whom the Lord killed because of a vague incident of "coitus interruptus" (an action for preventing fertilization) when Onan was having intercourse with his dead brother's wife. The passage is really about power, assets, and status within the tribe of Judah and is not related to a moral injunction for Christians to follow. Church teaching on masturbation, described as a form of ipsation (self-gratification),[47] is also based on Romans 1:26, where Paul describes other deviant forms of sexuality as seriously evil. In tradition, the church has always held such acts as impure and unchaste and has classified them as "mortally sinful," worthy of eternal condemnation. What has happened in today's world is the Christian's refusal to put any credence in what the church says on the matter. Chastity and purity are valued virtues in any life status, be it single or married. However, to legislate that masturbation is impure, unchaste, and sinful is to go beyond reason for the educated Christian, and it no longer ought to be a matter that the church should legislate upon to any extent. I would suggest that the inquirer make use of the science of psychology to discover a healthier outlook on the matter. There is no better way to inform one's conscience for decision-making than to expand and allow science to enter in and cleanse one's mind of ancient and harmful religious legislation.

Premarital Sex

To begin this discussion, I would like to quote a declaration of the Catholic Church relating to conjugal relationships.

> Experience teaches us that love must find its safeguard in the stability of marriage, if sexual intercourse is truly to respond to the requirements of its own finality and to those of human dignity. These requirements call for a conjugal contract sanctioned and guaranteed by society, a contract which establishes a state of life of importance both for the exclusive union of the man and the woman and for the good of their family and of the human community. Most often, in fact, premarital relations exclude the possibility of children. What is represented to be conjugal love is not able, as it absolutely should be, to develop into paternal and maternal love. Or, if it does happen to do so, this will be to the detriment of the children, who will be deprived of the stable environment in which they ought to develop in order to find in it the way and the means of their insertion into society as a whole. The consent given by people who wish to be united in marriage must therefore be manifested externally and in a manner which makes it valid in the eyes of society. As far as the faithful are concerned, their consent to the setting up of a community of conjugal life must be expressed according to the laws of the Church. It is a consent which makes their marriage a Sacrament of Christ. *(Declaration of the Sacred Congregation Concerning Sexual Ethics*, 1975)

It is important to look carefully at the excerpt from the Sacred Congregation for the Doctrine of the Faith. This declaration, called *Persona Humana*, represents closely what all prelates from Pope Leo IX (1054) onward have declared, up to the present time. The Catholic Church has been very consistent over the centuries in establishing its place in determining just what constitutes and grounds a marital relationship. The translation into English is well done and well written, well worth reading, and upon scrutiny, anyone can see how the Catholic Church made these statements from a particular stance.

At this point, it is my intent to explain where the thinking behind the encyclical sinks much like a boat taking on water. Some serious questions surface:

1. What experience tells us that love finds ultimate stability in marriage?

2. What law of nature tells us that progeny must always be the finality of sexual intercourse?

3. In marriage, why must the union always be between man and woman?

4. What research tells us that same-sex partners cannot raise a stable and healthy family?

5. Why is it not possible for common-law unions to raise stable and healthy families?

6. To be faithful to Christ, why is following the defined church laws always essential?

7. On what basis does the Catholic Church define how children are to be conceived?

Other topics, such as primary purpose of marriage and homosexuality (covered later in this chapter), also enter into the debate.

The excerpt from the encyclical has value in that it preaches an
ideal. Aside from the possibility that such an ideal might not
exist, we can still say it is noble to preach something that aspires
to some kind of higher order of things. The ideal is that sexual
activity among couples ought to be taking place within a forever
commitment. If sex is only for making babies, then couples who
conceive need to protect the baby within a protective relationship.

In Old Testament times and well into Christian tradition, a teenage culture did not exist, only girls and boys who lived and performed their duties under their parents' supervision. Oftentimes,
if teenagers paired off for a walk or enjoyed a simple friendship,
they were more than likely placed in a prearranged betrothal
situation, with variations of this "locked-in" approach being determined by different cultural practices. Adulterers and unwed
mothers were either hidden away (within the domain of a male
elder, possibly as a second/third wife), or murdered outright with
members of the community looking on in passive approval. The
way society at the time taught its young people was under the
specter of absolute fear of reprisal, not forgiveness and acceptance.
It was "Live your lives as your parents do, or else." A contradiction
here, which many miss, is that most of the great leaders in biblical
history had multiple wives and multiple mistresses, bearing many
offspring. Fidelity in a monogamous relationship, even in Jesus's
time, was not as common as one might think. When the Pharisees
confronted Jesus about Mosaic law allowing a man to divorce his
wife, Jesus's response was more than likely given to protect the

wife, who was considered chattel of the husband, oppressed and possessing few or no rights.[48]

Given the static view of moral edicts of the Old Testament, one can see how the celibate rabbi St. Paul (a major contributor to the Church's theological stance) would be influential in determining what should happen in an ideal world. St. Paul, a wonderful preacher and advocate for the Christian community, had difficulty with the whole concept of sexuality. In some instances, he preached from the order of divine law. Then, in other instances, he preached from his own belief about certain sexual behaviors. The problem for the inquirer is to figure out which hat he was wearing at the time.

In 1 Corinthians chapter 7, Paul speaks of the problem of justifying any new state in life, seeing the "end time" was near. Understanding what Paul preached within the early community is essential for grasping Pauline concepts on human sexuality. In modern times, the challenge is to see how closely connected coitus is to the promise of commitment in marriage. Love and commitment have been, and will continue to be, in marriage vows. However, what we understand in history as the marriage act (coitus) carries a different connotation today. People learn about love in a variety of ways. One would think coitus means an act of commitment on the part of the couple, but reality says that is not always the case today. Research done in a Catholic college in 2008 indicates that 70 percent of church-going Catholics do not believe the Bible or Christian teaching on sexuality. Among Catholics who do not attend church, the number is even higher, 86 percent.[49]

Looking at the advice and insights on sexual behavior that the church has offered over the centuries, one can consider her teaching precepts as an ideal, an admirable goal for young and old, men and women alike. All things being equal, it would be good to remain virginal until a community can authenticate the vows of marriage, but I cannot say that this is a verifiable bit of advice. I would like to believe it. However, there is no evidence in modern society that virginal couples married in front of a community of believers are any more successful in their commitment as life partners than those who have had several relationships prior to marriage. In fact, a significant percentage (30–45 percent) of Christian and non-Christian marriages end up in some form of dissolution and/or divorce. The modern believer could very well ask why the church has not moved itself out of the bedrooms of the Christian faithful. The church's response to that question is that its doctrinal teachings and Catholic tradition actually have something to say. I believe the church does have something to say regarding a healthy sexuality, but, given the results of research provided, the church needs to broaden its view on sexuality and make these statements less often. The basis upon which the church has made pronouncements does not allow a different position on sexuality. Premarital sex as evil and punishable by eternal fire is simply nonsense and is overworked by religious institutions. Such a position must and will change over time.

The Paranormal

Over the last century, there has been much ado about strange portents occurring within Christian and non-Christian communities. There are possession by spirits, instances of witchcraft, and presently, the extraordinary exorcist narratives. These expose an amazingly bizarre world of the unexplainable. It is not my intent to delve into the depths of discussion about any of stories that have surfaced, but rather, to clarify how it is possible to evaluate such phenomena when they occur.

Most people are attracted to the world of the mysterious and unusual. When some kind of coincidence or unusual story comes our
way, we focus on the unexplainable facts of the incident. It is in
our nature to attempt to explain, in a physical way, why something
happened. The less understandable the thing is, the more we hold
on to it as a quasi-supernatural phenomenon. This experience may
come with a conviction that there is a spiritual entity or power at
the source of the experience.

We can learn a great deal from a discussion of the paranormal. The
word can denote the power of telekinesis or clairvoyance that is beyond the scope of scientific understanding, or a mystic who believes
he has special powers.[50] To be honest, I have never seen a drinking
glass rise up from a table, except when I was a child and my uncle
pulled a trick on us young ones. We could not explain what happened for quite some time. The paranormal and pseudo-supernatural
phenomena appear to fall outside of scientific investigation, but science is always interested in explaining phenomena that carry some
physical reality and potential explanation.

There are those who discuss the paranormal in the same breath
as the supernatural, almost as if the two words were synonyms.
Research indicates that the use of the word *paranormal* originated
about the 1920s, whereas the use of the word *supernatural* dates
back as early as the fifteenth century CE.[51] We can describe
the paranormal as experiences not yet explained by science. The
supernatural, however lies outside the realm of scientific verifica-
tion. As long as we separate the two considerations, the paranormal and supernatural, we can arrive at some sort of satisfaction
for our inquiring minds.

I can recall, as a child, seeing ghosts moving in my bedroom and
never once considering that the moonlight shining through the

window was casting a moving image through the curtain and onto the wall. Although this experience was not clairvoyant, I wanted to see a ghost. Sometimes what one believes to happen will happen. We have much to learn about the power of the mind and its capabilities. The future could be very exciting for anyone interested in the paranormal.

Treating some personal experience as supernatural is a different matter. It would be something similar to a miracle in the traditional sense. It is my belief that the more we attribute strange phenomena to a supernatural or religious source, the less we want to explain it as physically caused. It is unfortunate to say God did it, because doing so allows superstition to be the driver of our thoughts and conclusions. As we grow older with this way of thinking, it is almost impossible to be convinced otherwise. Miraculous cures are just one example of this unfortunate tendency, as we automatically attribute to some divine intervention the reason for a sudden change in our health.

Homosexuality and Related Issues

Western civilization is rapidly accepting and accommodating homosexuality and gay marriage, especially in areas where populations are dense and Western democracy flourishes. This is not the case in other parts of the world, starting with areas of the Middle East, and most Pacific Rim countries under strict religious control. In past centuries, Christendom has not exhibited any notable respect for gays and lesbians. In fact, there are numerous instances of public persecutions, burning at the stake, and other abominable measures taken to rid communities of "abnormal and sinful activity."

The Catholic Church has stated in more recent times the need for compassion for homosexuals, not condemning the person, but the activity.[52] Such a position does little to alleviate the challenges faced by this community. In the past, we understood homosexuality as abnormal. That was a mistake. Today, science understands homosexuality as an "atypical condition." We notice such behavior in many mammalian populations. Within members of a wolf pack, there are individuals who never mate but are caretakers and providers for younger members. Among the primates, scientists have found young males coupling and apparently not introduced into the reproductive population.

Humans and most animals live and reproduce in a dimorphic world. That is to say, there are two sexes, and two sexes are necessary to continue and preserve the species. Male and female coupling is typical behavior in animals. Coupling of the same sex of a species is atypical, but not abnormal in the pejorative sense, since a certain percentage of most species exhibit this atypical behavior. Recent medical and genetic research has shown that matters relating to the XX and the XY typical classification of the sex chromosomes are not all clear-cut. There are anomalies resulting in individuals being neither male nor female. An example would be the SRY gene. How this gene functions will determine the type of sexuality. We could say the same thing about the absence or overabundance of maternal estrogens during fetal development in the womb.

It is not my intent at this time to elaborate to any extent the advances that science has made relating to sexuality. My intent is to point out that male and female behavior is not so predictable. It is not that human sexuality has changed, but rather, our understanding of sexuality has greatly improved due to science. The following represents a nonprofessional explanation for people who are very interested but are not equipped with background knowledge derived from research in science. A recent *National Graphic* article offers us a good description of what science informs us on this topic. The following is an excerpt:

> Today we know that the various elements of what we consider "male" and "female" don't always line up neatly, with all the XXs—complete with ovaries, vagina, estrogen, female gender identity, and feminine behavior—on one side, and all the XYs—testes, penis, testosterone, male gender identity, and masculine behavior—on the other. It's possible to be XX and mostly male in terms of anatomy, physiology, and psychology, just as it's possible to be XY and mostly female.
>
> … Sex differentiation is usually set in motion by a gene on the Y chromosome, the SRY gene that makes the proto-gonads turn into testes … Without the SRY gene, the proto-gonads become ovaries that secrete estrogen, and the fetus develops female anatomy (uterus, vagina, and clitoris).
>
> But the SRY gene's function isn't always straightforward. The gene might be missing or dysfunctional, leading to an XY embryo that fails to develop male anatomy and is identified at birth as a girl. Or it might show up on the X chromosome, leading to an XX embryo that does develop male anatomy and is identified at birth as a boy.
>
> Genetic variations can occur that are unrelated to the SRY gene, such as complete androgen insensitivity syndrome (CAIS), in which an XY embryo's cells respond minimally, if at all, to the signals of

male hormones. Even though the proto-gonads become testes and the fetus produces androgens, male genitals don't develop. The baby looks female, with a clitoris and vagina, and in most cases will grow up feeling herself to be a girl. Which is this baby, then? Is she the girl she believes herself to be? Or, because of her XY chromosomes—not to mention the testes in her abdomen—is she "really" male?[53]

It would benefit the reader to research the advancements made by the science of epigenetics[54] and its study on development of the human body and sexuality. Although we think we know the difference between a male and a female through external observations, we make judgments based on the expectation of typical behaviors and fail to realize the presence of natural atypical behaviors in our world. A simple explanation of hermaphroditism (both sex organs present) as an aberration of nature does injustice to the reality of what is found in nature. Recent research indicates that about one in a hundred individuals falls into the intersex mix of male and female chromosomes, testicular and ovarian tissues, genitals, and other sexual characteristics.[55]

Let us now look at homosexuality, related LGTBQ[56] issues, and the predictable spin-off we call gay marriage. It is my belief that the good news of Jesus Christ has been construed to fit in with the ancient and questionable teachings of Jews and Christians. Jesus's episode with the woman supposedly caught in adultery[57] can encourage the believer to understand Jesus's attempts to be loving, compassionate, forgiving, and respectful toward the downtrodden and persecuted ones in Israel. It is difficult, given all the redactions of the text, to determine the exact words of Jesus, but without a doubt, the spirit of the confrontation with the onlookers indicates some important moral truths Jesus was teaching. It is that we should be compassionate and forgiving to those who find themselves caught up in an apparent violation of norms of conduct. Stoning of women accused of adultery was the norm of conduct at the time. Jesus's response to the accusers was to say, "He who is without sin cast the first stone." There was no science as an ally to support anyone who might be different and no judges present to make sure the penalty was commensurate with the crime. We can now consider some insights into the modern believer's action on LGTBQ issues.

Society must give all the support and tolerance needed to live in this world as true human beings. Groups of individuals who are atypical with their intersex and behavioral characteristics need acceptance. Intersex individuals (biological with both physical sex organs) and androgynous individuals (gender expression and identity included) deserve, under the law, the same respect and rights that typical males and females are being afforded. At present, we have little knowledge of the effects of hormones, nutrients, medications, and other chemical substances in the womb. We do know such influences sometimes result in atypical behavior. The mind is at least in part what the brain does. If structures in the brain change in any way, the mind and consequent behaviors will display atypical conditions, but these are not abnormal conditions. As a result, when discussing rights of these individuals under democratic law, we should honor all claims like marriage and other types of unions. Unfortunately, atypical males and females become the target of discrimination because they are not exactly like us. This is what Jesus was protesting during His public life. The only way Jesus can continue the work He did during His public life is by working through the minds and hearts of Christians today. Forgiveness, compassion, respect, and acceptance in our hearts become the mandate. Those who confront this direct and personal discrimination are actually the faces of Jesus and the voices of God in our world.

Although there are many other issues that could be discussed, basic ideas and principles have been offered that illustrate one's need to constantly evaluate where to draw the line on religious practices and teachings. Now is the time for the modern Christian believer to redirect through positive actions the original inspirations and teaching of Jesus Christ. More important than any proclamations emanating from a religious group on moral matters is the informed conscience taking on the personality of Christ. The often-quoted phrase of ancient Jewish scholars that Jesus used, "Do unto others as you would have them do unto you," should never be diluted by any proclamations that lessen its application. Justice will prevail, at least in its basic intent, if Christians take to heart this basic message of Jesus.

9

Ceremony and Ritual: Outward Expressions of Faith

In this chapter, I will treat the nature of specific Christian ceremonies and rituals. Ceremonies and rituals are celebrations that constantly evolve with influence from the cultural practices of the day. However, there are some ceremonies that curtail the development of modern belief. Christmas and Easter are excellent examples of faith-enhancing celebrations, but they also contain aspects that are of questionable value today. Sacraments will be treated with the respect they deserve, while, at the same time, being shown to exhibit some applications of outdated and irrelevant theological beliefs. The reader may ask, why this chapter? My response is that ceremonies and rituals are where the evolution of religious practices and belief take place, at the grassroots level.

The following is a list of definitions that generally relate to when we gather as a group. Although these terms are discussed within the appropriate sections, I choose to initially define them as a starting point in understanding what lies ahead in this chapter. Not all Christians hold exactly the same understanding of some basic religious terms, and I acknowledge this fact.

1. Ceremony: A formal or symbolic act or observance, or a series of acts, as on religious and state occasions. The doing of some formal act in the manner prescribed by authority or usage.[58]

2. Ritual: A prescribed form or method for the performance of a religious or solemn ceremony; a body of rites or ceremonies. Ritualism is a system of conducting public worship according to prescribed or established forms.[59]

3. Rite: A solemn or religious ceremony performed in an established or prescribed manner, or the words or acts constituting or accompanying it. Any formal practice or custom.[60]

4. Symbol: Something chosen to stand for or represent something else, usually because of a resemblance in qualities or characteristics; an object used to typify a quality, an abstract idea.[61] For example, partaking of the Eucharist symbolizes the unity of Christians into one bread and one body (1 Corinthians 10:17).

5. Sign: A representation of any sort used to indicate something.[62] For example, the Eucharist is an effective sign of Christian unity, made so by the church being the body of Christ.[63]

In our daily routines, we all have ways of doing things. For example, for me (perhaps because I am right-handed) it is difficult to put on a shirt when placing my left arm into the sleeve first.

We can say the same about social interactions. There is a story of a man who takes regular walks in a nearby park. Occasionally, he comes upon an elderly man sitting in the same place on a park bench most days. Sitting down beside him, he strikes up a conversation. After a bit of small talk, he asks him about his routine of sitting in the same place on the bench. His response was, "I sit in this same place on the bench each day because I feel more comfortable. You know, when you are my age, you need to recognize where you are, and, for me, this helps me remember where I have been. I have done it before, and I'll know exactly what I will do when it is time for me to get up and go." After saying this, he looks at his watch and says, "It's time for me to go—good day!" It was probably an amazing experience for the questioner. It is much like Tevye when, in *Fiddler on the Roof,* he expounded on the importance of tradition. Performing some things as a routine is crucial in establishing confidence and satisfaction in our lives. Such activity grounds us and gives us a sense of stability. The topics to be treated in this chapter are a constant reminder that as we grow older and take on more responsibility, there is confidence and a sense of security that not only do we grow personally, but also grow socially in relationships with others who share the same needs and beliefs.

Celebrations Are for Everyone

Celebrations have been a key factor in defining human nature and are a unique and distinguishing hallmark of our species. When a group of any size comes together to mark an event, there is usually a reason to celebrate. In religious ceremonies, attention is paid to landmark events that seem important for survival of the group. A ceremony often accompanies a public event; it may include a formal proclamation of rejoicing or even mourning the loss of someone. A ritual, on the other hand can be a prescribed form or method for the performance of a ceremony. The further one re-searches the origin of ceremonies and ancient practices, the more religious in nature they appear to be. It is also important to distin-guish customs from ceremony and ritual, since customs indicate a much broader understanding of ways of doing or accomplishing something, including the minor acts of a cultural group or na-tion. Customs in the secular world always evolve more rapidly than religious ones. Let us first look at the two most important celebrations in Christianity, the feasts of Christmas and Easter.

Christmas Is a Universal Favorite

I have yet to meet anyone of any faith, or no faith at all, who does not find the Christmas season at least somewhat enjoyable. There are two parallel themes always present when celebrating Christ's birth. The first theme is quite traditional and features eleventh-century Franciscan modifications to the crib,[64] coupled with other, earlier contributions to the nativity scene, such as the shepherds, the magi, and the star of Bethlehem. The second theme, which penetrates deeply into most Christian denomina-tions, is the appearance of "jolly ol' St. Nick," the giver of good gifts. This gentleman-saint has morphed into a happy figure, now often located in most large department stores, either giving out gifts or asking for financial support for a good cause. So deeply rooted into Western society is Christmas that holiday time, trav-elling time, and gift-giving make it the greatest type of economic boost ever to happen to modern cities and countries. Both the themes of the nativity and of Santa Claus are here to stay for a long time as events worthy of celebration. Although one theme is religious in nature and the other secular, in most countries, there is a very compatible coexistence evident. Those promoting the religious theme will always complain about Christ being absent from Christmas, but they fail to realize that there were constant changes and expressions made to the story of Christmas during the first five centuries in all areas around the Middle East.

Many changes have taken place since the first century. The early Christians apparently did not focus on the details of Christ's birth. However, by the fourth century, Christians celebrated Christ's Mass as a replacement feast for the winter solstice and the ancient feasts of Roman and Greek gods. The Savior's birth, along with the feast of the annunciation (nine months prior), were important testimonial celebrations that emphasized to the faithful that Jesus was truly human. The Christ Child came into the world as truly human as well as divine. This approach was intended to dispel any similarities to the origin of gods and demigods. The humanity of Jesus carried with it all the descriptions expected of an individual born helpless, yet endearing. What has happened over the last five centuries is an interaction between the religious and secular themes that could prove fruitful. Gift-giving near the winter solstice is as ancient as most religions. However, Jesus as savior is the new gift given for all to enjoy. Consequently, just as we have been given Christ as savior, we can also give gifts and be gifts for others. Christmas should be a personal experience rather than just a memory to be celebrated. It is my belief that there are other nuances to the meaning of Christmas. The experience of young parents is that a baby changes everything. In turn, all of us can wait in expectation that we can be born anew and be a gift for others.

The point and purpose here are to take interest in local and regional expressions of the Christmas season, which is a season filled with real gift-giving experiences. Genuine expression of what a gift might be should generate an open and a unifying experience for the Christian. A valid expression will be the one that has perennial acceptance.

Easter as the Final Act of Surrender

The Holy Triduum of Easter is the most important celebration for all Christians. Holy Thursday, Good Friday, and Holy Saturday represent Jesus's final act of surrender to His mission in the world. Through commemoration of His suffering, death, and resurrection, Christians experience, in some way, Jesus's suffering and death so that they, too, might be with Him on the last day. The ceremonies for these special days are extraordinary, with rituals that truly reflect many cultural themes. There is no doubt that Easter will be the center point of all Christian worship as long as there is allowance for productive changes.

The liturgical celebrations of Easter may have varied somewhat in different regions in the Roman Empire. There is some question as to the timing of the events of Palm Sunday, which may have occurred during the fall celebration of the Feast of Tabernacles, and the possibility that the arrest of Jesus took place earlier than three days before Easter. Nonetheless, Friday is probably the day of the week Christ died.[65] One could question the accuracy of the passion of Jesus, how it took place, and specific events leading up to the road to Calvary, but few Christians today deny that Jesus's suffering and death took place. Christians will always discuss the need for such a death, but that Jesus did suffer and die will continue to be an essential belief, filled with many types of rituals and ceremonies. For the early Christian community (predominantly Jewish), the connection between the prophecies in Jewish tradition and the passion and death of Jesus was crucial for the teaching and preaching of the early disciples. Although we could validly question the accuracy of Old Testament application to Jesus, there is no doubt that His life and death did happen.

The events following Jesus's resurrection are questionable in terms of accuracy. Most scholars maintain that each devotional group developed its own testimonial assertions as to how the postresurrected Jesus presented himself. Hence, rituals took on a variety of expressions in the early years of the church. It is not until a few centuries later that resurrection narratives were set in place for all to accept as the official canon (New and Old Testament writings). What is interesting to note is, although these celebrations of both Christmas and Easter are of paramount importance, they have changed and will continue to change as a form of adaptation to the needs and thoughts of the time.

Sacraments and Sacramentals

It is true that the Catholic understanding of the terms *sacrament* and *sacramental* originated within the Catholic Church, but they also exist under different names in most other Christian denominations after the Reformation years of the fifteenth and sixteenth centuries. At this point, I will focus on those sacraments and sacramentals that elicit some contentious challenges for the modern believer. It is at the grassroots level that religious beliefs grow and develop. For the common believer, the sacraments become focal points in a personal expression of faith within a Christian community.

A sacrament is defined as an outward sign, instituted by Christ, to bring grace into our soul.[66] Investigating what is behind this statement is not my objective here, but I invite the reader to research the sophisticated meanings behind each word of this definition. Jesus never used the term *sacrament*, although there are indications in the letters of the apostles that there had been a common understanding. The word *sacrament* evolved from Roman tradition, which, among other things, was a form of legal settlement among citizens. Regardless, the Christian community understood the nature of these special ceremonies, and there were some ceremonies considered more important than others. The rituals involved in all ceremonies differed noticeably during the first three centuries.

The Sacraments of Initiation

For centuries, Christians held baptism, confirmation, and the Holy Eucharist as rituals that conducted the candidate into a new experience in the faith. They are crucial for developing faith as a living experience. Baptism represents being born into the new life of Jesus, a new life offered to all, infants and adults alike. Confirmation in modern times is the extension of the baptismal experience, with emphasis on issuing the believer into an adult witness to the good news of Jesus Christ. In many countries, the presider often administers them at the same time.

In many non-Catholic denominations, baptism is administered when the aspirant has reached the age of reason or even adulthood. The first two sacraments of initiation will always be valid outward signs and rituals that, in some form, introduce us into the life of Christ in a believing community. The sacrament of the Holy Eucharist issues from the ancient Christian rite of breaking bread and sharing the cup. As an act of giving thanks, partaking in the supper of the Lord meant that believers were in solidarity with their community and the Christian community at large. Performing the rite of breaking bread does not take place at all religious gatherings. Upon the occasion of special solemnities and feasts adhered to by many denominations of protestant origin, the sharing of bread, along with wine or grape juice, does take place. In the Catholic, Episcopal, and Anglican Churches, one can find definite preparations prior to the administering of the bread and wine at Holy Mass. An individual would, when properly prepared, receive the Holy Eucharist, the third sacrament of initiation.

At this time, I wish to focus on the total ceremonial ritual of the Mass, which Catholics call the Eucharistic celebration. For two thousand years, the Mass has been the source of many conflicts and divisions; it has been the ceremony most altered and most radically changed from the practice and spiritual thought of the early Christians. When one shares in the breaking of the bread in a religious community, the act of taking bread assumes that all present share the common beliefs of that community. The challenge today is that there are too many beliefs expected of the communicant, and the perception of being in total union with the person in the pew next to you becomes blurred and many times lost.

The Magician and the Magic

In Matthew's gospel, we have Jesus saying that where two or three are gathered in His name, there He is with them.[67] A memorial supper became the focal point of Jesus's presence, because Jesus did not return to restore a new kingdom in a traditional way. Furthermore, at that time, there were no readings except from Jewish manuscripts and Old Testament references about the promised Messiah, the savior of Israel. This sharing of the word occurred when the breaking of the bread took place. Toward the end of the first century, many accounts of Jesus's life, along with shared letters from the early disciples, were read and treasured as accounts of someone who changed believers' lives forever. These latter manuscripts became important prayerful and instructional materials. The term *Mass* originated from the presider sending the believer from the worshiping congregation using the Latin phrase "Ite, missa est" ("Go, it is sent"). The phrase, used as a dismissal to those who attended the religious ceremony, morphed into the word *Mass*, which is still used today.

Over the centuries, liturgical scholars have outlined the evolution of the ceremonies and rituals of the last supper of our Lord. The purpose of this discussion is to show what aspects of the Holy Eucharistic celebration surface as questionable—in need of evaluation and change to meet the needs of the believing Christian today. In the early Middle Ages, the separation of the presider (priest in this ceremony) from the worshipping community became evident, with priestly ceremonies and rituals taking place at a high altar, set apart from the people by a railing at which the consecrated bread was distributed. The consecration of unleavened bread became the central point of the Holy Mass. Although Catholic Church theologians maintain that the liturgy of the Word is as important as the liturgy of the Eucharist, in practice this is not the case. The consecration portion of the liturgy of the Eucharist still is the most solemn ritual inside the ceremony of Holy Mass. There could be several reasons for this, and I will treat just one because it clearly shows why there is a need for today's Christian to reevaluate the theology behind the ritual.

For about fifteen hundred years, the church has insisted that the very words spoken at the consecration meant, at that instant, the bread and wine were transformed into the very body and blood of the resurrected Jesus Christ. Only a priest could perform this function, and although the items retained the outward appearances of bread and wine, in faith the Christian was consuming the body and blood of Jesus. St Thomas Aquinas (twelfth century CE) solidified this belief by philosophically convincing the teaching church that what is a matter of faith could also be an actual reality. It is not my intent to delve into concepts relating to the nature of the Eucharist in this work. Concepts such as transubstantiation, essence, and substance are constructs of a philosophy using the traditional thoughts of Plato and Aristotle. The mistake in such an approach is to take a matter of faith that is theoretically conceivable and posit it as a physical reality. St. Thomas preached this very notion. However, raising the host above the head at the consecration, as such, is not a matter of reality to be verified but a matter to be believed.

What makes this traditional thought even more challenging is the expansion of the concept of the bread as an object worthy of adoration. This is what happens when the host is part of a ritual parade within a church or out on the street. The Catholic Church calls this ritual a sacramental action. All of this type of thinking has at its source the questionable traditional belief of the priest's special powers. Critics have had a field day with the magical work of the priest at the time of the Eucharistic consecration. The Eucharistic celebration is not magic performed by a magician, but the church has done nothing to soften this erroneous belief or to dispel an accusation that Catholics are none other than spiritual cannibals. To refute these accusations would require a radically different approach to the celebration of the Eucharist. I would like to propose the following liturgical changes and the thoughts behind them.

The liturgical movements during the Mass need to be rebalanced and refocused. Liturgists need to place more emphasis on the first part of the presentation of the gifts, including the bread and wine being set aside, and less emphasis on the consecration portion of the Eucharistic celebration. In addition, liturgists need to place more emphasis on the liturgy of the Word as being the very presence of Jesus at our gathering. Early Christians talked about the importance of the Word, but even today, a Sunday obligation is still met when one arrives too late to partake in the Word. It is okay as long as the parishioner is in place in time to respond to the collection basket! The second Vatican council initiated a very positive direction for refocusing the liturgy of the Word and

Eucharist from the priestly activity to the presence of the contemporary worshipping community.

In recent times, there appears to be a return to former Tridentine thought through the reinsertion of some medieval rituals, with even Latin reappearing once again in the vocal responses from the congregation. The insertion of archaic terms into the vocal responses is totally out of place. For example, the placement of "consubstantial" into the Nicene Creed represents a regression back into the verbiage of the Thomistic era of the eleventh century. These additions fail to enhance the faith experience of the believer. Concerning Jesus's relationship with the Father, it is obtuse enough with the original wording "one in being with the Father." Now, with a reinsertion of words like *consubstantial* and other medieval concepts, the move to centralize the congregation as the important factor of worship has been derailed.

It is my belief that evolution of Christian belief has challenges when the Catholic Church insists on emphasizing differences in rituals and ceremonies rather than similarities. The church made mistakes by insisting that the priest, at the time of the consecration, has some kind of magical powers, while being clothed with ostentatious garments. Whereas the presence of Christ in a religious celebration is experienced in the very act of communicating the Word, bread, and wine. The reading of scripture produces the power of the good news. Similarly, the blessing, breaking, and sharing of the bread and wine with the believer becomes the power of the sacramental presence, not the words of the presider of the ceremony. Jesus made it very clear when He said, "Where two or three are gathered in my name, there I am." It is just a matter of time before the idea of being in communion with each other at Mass will once again become the real focal point of the Eucharist.

At the beginning of this chapter, I quoted Fr. John McKenzie, SJ, who stated, "the Body of Christ is the Church, and this makes the Eucharist the effective sign of Christian unity." There is a difference between effective sign and a reality. Non-Catholic denominations have been maintaining this stance for some centuries now. The challenge now is to set up a ceremony that clearly points out that the church is the body of Christ, and that the sharing of bread and wine is truly an act of "comm-unity" of the believers with one another.

Over the last four centuries, the non-Catholic denominations have taken the lead in allowing a liturgy to be truly the work of the people, rather than the prescription of a higher authority. Catholic liturgists fear the possibility that the Mass will become a memorial service and not a reenactment of the saving power of Jesus's life, death, and resurrection. Christ is indeed present in the ceremony, just as the church is the body of Christ. However, bread and wine are only the symbolic body and blood of Christ, which is now the church. If church authorities cannot move ahead and adapt to more realistic faith experiences, similar to what I have proposed, modern believers will discard traditional beliefs and practices as foundation for a banquet table that fewer and fewer people attend.

Sacraments of Healing

The sacraments of reconciliation and the anointing of the sick are wonderful expressions of ceremonial acts within the Christian community. These ceremonial practices have been and will continue to be part of the saving acts of the Holy Spirit because they find their origin and power in the believing Christian. It is true that the traditional church has taught and still teaches that there is a causal effect produced in part by the administrator of a ceremony. In the next chapter, we discuss the value placed on the placebo effect in the medical sciences and the research on that subject. We recognize the power of forgiveness and healing in almost all aspects of our lives, from birth to death. Although on the right track for realizing the power of the mind to bring about a variety of changes, much has yet to be learned about how neural and biochemical interactions generate healing on the emotional and purely physical levels.

Reconciliation

The Christian knows this ceremony as the sacrament of confession or penance, and it occurred in monastic communities during the Middle Ages.[68] Monastic control over forms of piety was probably closer to the real cause of the change from Christ's directive to go to the victim for forgiveness and reconciliation. "Whose sins you forgive, they are forgiven, and whose sins you retain, they are retained" is widely acknowledged as a postresurrection insertion into manuscripts, produced by the early disciples when the Christian communities were being formed. Nonetheless, the use of some public act of absolution within a developing community offered a remarkable form of healing and well-being, particularly in times when court systems were either nonexistent or woefully inadequate for those who were illiterate, uneducated, and vulnerable to the dictators of the time.

Scholastics indicate that initial public confessions occurred once during one's life, or when, in a special instance, the community experienced harm done by an individual.[69] The anointing of the sick (last rites) was also associated with the forgiveness of sins and was administered at the time of death. The introduction of personal confession appears to be associated with the early practices of monastic life. It is this type of confession of sins and forgiveness that later became what we understand as the confessional experience. Forgiveness of sins was the prerogative of the presiding elder (assumed to be a priest), along with the role of celebrant at the breaking of the bread. The lesser offices of the subdeaconate and deaconate were in place for assisting in handling other, more specific needs of the community.

As monastic life evolved and became the focal point of education and religious life in the church, certain practices found to be fruitful for the religious-minded, such as private confession, quickly became a mainstay for the education and control of the moral lives of uneducated believers. What we have today is an overexpansion and proliferation of restrictions upon the confessor as to how he can give absolution for a particular violation (sin). One would think that during childhood, the parent would absolve and administer forgiveness, since the mother and father are the true presence of the forgiving God in the Christian family. Unfortunately, such is not the case today. The Catholic Church has persisted in the rote practice of weekly and monthly confession as an ideal for the child, isolating the parent as if he or she was not fit to administer the sacrament of reconciliation. Once the child reaches adulthood, there is a drastic reduction in the use of reconciliation. Monastic life is truly on the wane, and the level of education of the confessor simply does not measure up to the needs of the educated modern believer. The private confession of sins may have a value, as it did for the monks in the early times of the church, but for the contemporary believer, its importance is becoming less and less obvious.

Anointing of the Sick

The last rites have been and continue to be an expression of Christian love for the helpless and aged members in a community.

What makes the rite very important and relevant is not a particular ritual or ceremony involved, but rather the evoking of a special power from within those who are sick or aged. The power of the mind is beyond comprehension, and the placebo effect could definitely bring about special healing from this sacrament. The power of the sacrament comes not just from the minister, but also from the acceptance of the ritual due to the faith of the believer. If one remembers, even Christ could not work miracles in communities where doubt and skepticism prevailed.[70] Transferal of the powers of healing and well-being from the minister to the recipient does not rule out the importance of both parties, i.e., both the priest and penitent or ailing recipient. This relationship is integral for accomplishing the healing the power of Christ.

The image figure of Christ elicits amazing conversion and healing properties within the recipient. The powers from within a penitent heart can work wonders by visualizing the Christ figure in the priest or layperson who administers the sacrament. Some actions, such as laying on of hands, are healing factors in health and well-being and can result in a sense of forgiveness. We could discuss much more about the sacrament of healing at this point, but suffice it to say, belief in healing on all levels will continue to be important to the Christian. However, as time goes by, the idea that there has been a magical act and that the administrator is a magician will play a diminishing role in the Christian community.

Sacraments of Vocation

Scholars believe matrimony and holy orders are the two final outward signs instituted by Christ. These sacred ceremonial rituals fill out the seven rites, which represent a perfect number of seven. The church has long taught that having seven sacraments means that Christ has entered totally in the believer's life in all aspects and that, just as in biblical tradition, where seven represents a quasi-infinite number, so also the seven sacraments represent the fact that Jesus and His saving power have encompassed all needs for the Christian. The sacraments of vocation represent an important calling to a way of life. This is not to say that people who do not marry or become priests are incomplete in some way. In Christian tradition, these two ways of living form a framework within which the vast majority of people fulfill themselves in community. In the future, there may very well be a sacrament for the ones who do not wish to be married or enter the priesthood, but at present, this is what exists. In tradition, the two sacraments are in juxtaposition, a position that meant the mutual exclusion of each other. Of course, this belief only exemplified prejudice against women, which was common in all societies in early times. The Christian church was no different. Celibacy for the priest, although an ancient practice, is looked upon today as rather archaic, just as priesthood for men alone and not for women is incomplete and will never stand the test of time. Almost all Christian protestant denominations have rid themselves of such practices. In the course of the evolution of Christian belief, women will rightly find their place as formal purveyors of the good news of Jesus Christ and the breaking of the bread.

Matrimony

The Catholic Church did it correctly when it formally defined the sacrament of matrimony by the twelfth century CE.[71] The administrators (chief witnesses) of this sacrament are the newlyweds, expressing an undying love and commitment. In so doing, the couple sacramentally portrays the image of Christ's love for us. Jesus even said His Father's love for us is reflected in the committed love of a man and woman for each other.[72] The priest's function is to be solely a witness within the community, and that is it. The problem is that the church, probably for political reasons at the time, refused to stay out of the bedrooms of the faithful and held up as an ideal the absolute necessity of a forever commitment. Since such an expectation was unrealistic from the start, a great deal of legislation followed that detailed how, in the Catholic Church, such unions may be dissolved. Complicated processes followed, which may or may not have resolved the issues behind failed marriages and how second and even third marriages might be blessed within the church.

For many centuries, Catholics found their resolution to failed marriages within the legal framework of annulment. This required a structured legislative body (tribunal) to determine, for a variety of reasons, that there was never a real bond of commitment existing in the first place. At present, in Western society, annulments fall within secular governmental control as well. Without going into further discussion on this matter, the Catholic Church has burdened men and women with endless and confusing dictates relating to good and bad marriages, to the point that couples often feel it is better to live "in sin" than to break up a loving family structure.

Recently, Catholic Church pronouncements on the matter of bad marriages indicate a move to resolve the problem. In North America, the divorce rate for Catholics is approximately half the divorce rate in secular society. The concern here is that only 15 percent of Catholic couples in bad marriages actually complete an annulment process.[73] At this time, these couples do not participate fully in Catholic services. What started out in history to be the Catholic Church's practice to bless politically arranged unions for strengthening political alliances became a huge and major burden on local bishops at the grass roots level.[74]

Holy Orders

The sacrament of holy priesthood represents a crucial facet of cohesion in the Roman Catholic Church. With the anointing to the level of priesthood, the early Christian community set in place an authority (priesthood) that attempted to purvey a sense of continuity between the first disciples and authority figures in the surrounding regions of the Middle East. The institution of the subdeaconate, deaconate, and holy orders became part and parcel of the function of the presider at all the memorial services. Although they are generally understood to be offices restricted to men only, it is not clear that this was always the case. Regardless, from early on, the office of an appointed elder was to be male, and women's position in the synagogues was minor. The elder (male) in the early Christian community needed to be able to show the Jews at the time that Jesus was indeed the promised Messiah, the hope and aspiration of the local community and those potential converts from the Jewish Diaspora as well. Knowledge of the Torah and the other Old Testament manuscripts was crucial, since the vast majority of believers at the time were illiterate, not unlike religions elsewhere.

Church history spells out very well how the office of the priesthood has evolved. The image of the priest we have today was not that of the early Christian community. The office of the presider at services does indicate some essential similarities, such as a leader in praying and preaching the written or verbal words of the good news and the blessing, breaking, and sharing of the Eucharist (act of thanksgiving) within the memorial service. Otherwise, there is little in the priest's function that did not evolve from medieval times. Even the power of forgiveness given to the elders was shockingly different from how we understand the administering of the sacrament of reconciliation today. The scope of this work briefly shows how the evolution of the rituals and ceremonies of the church took place. Whether reasonable or not, the practices of a religious community were the product of a group of prelates and presbyters who needed to establish and maintain control and continuity with the traditions of the early fathers of the church.

Relating to the sacrament of the holy priesthood, there are some topics that, when looked at seriously, call for some major changes. The matter of ordination of women comes to the fore as an issue needing immediate attention. Protests continually surface regarding failure to live up to the needs of the time, a needed female parity with men in the church, and the lack of education of church officials and the faithful. Once the church has opened the door to woman priesthood, most will wonder why this did not happen a hundred years ago.

Although cultural traditions within the early Christian community would not tolerate a woman presider at gatherings, the Christian believer is ready for the change today and would do well by it. There are, at present, Catholic communities on our continent that enjoy this adaptation. The Vatican needs to move ahead on this just implementation as soon as possible. Most other non-Catholic denominations are doing well with women priests and ministers in their churches. Restrictions as to who can be ordained have nothing to do with dogma or matters of faith, but are simply a policy and practice from ancient and discriminatory traditions.

Another related topic is that of mandatory celibacy for the priesthood. Recall that celibacy is not the same as virginity or chastity. Although these three qualities can exist together, it is not always the case. Celibacy is a lifestyle that does not include marriage. It is my belief that many serious challenges the church faces today would greatly diminish if celibacy were to be optional for priests. It is a different world today, and the world we live in today will not revert to that of the early days of the church, where women were property instead of partners in life, work, and vocation. Situations such as those in South America, where ordained priests are cohabitating with life partners, need to be addressed immediately. A married priesthood should be approved all over the world. Our present pope Francis is well aware of the problem, to which there is only one beneficial course of action in South America, and that would be a married priesthood. The church needs to accommodate a married priesthood in order to eradicate a stigma that lies heavily upon a very dedicated and priestly group of men. The proper course of action would be to legitimize and bless these connubial unions.

Lastly, challenges surface with regard to pedophilia. The observer incorrectly believes this disorder relates to a celibate priesthood. In truth, such a vice occurs in all vocations in life. It raises its ugly head within the ministry because men with such proclivities tend to gather in situations where this crime of opportunity can more easily take place. This disorder surfaces in the priesthood, and many prelates are all too slow to curb and rectify the abuse. In addition, out of fear, family members hide the abuse in the home. Since this is the case, there is less likely to be a disclosure of molestation, and the abuse goes on.

In conclusion, we can say, having looked at ritual and ceremony as they occur in church services, that there will continue to be an outward expression of faith in a sacred way. This expression could be through momentous events celebrated or by means of acts directly related to what Jesus performed while He lived among us. Besides the sacraments, there are other actions and objects of lesser value that are somewhat disposable, such as sacramentals, which include medals, holy water, novenas, indulgences, blessings, and formal benedictions. These minor devotions could be helpful, as long as they are not manipulative and do not become objects of superstition.

When we realize what symbolism means, we can move forward and evaluate the ritual and ceremony properly. The use of symbol is real for the believer but is not itself the reality. A symbol represents something else. The bread and wine is the reality and can never change into body and blood (we are not cannibals). Our faith act verifies and symbolizes the presence of Jesus as the bread for a faith-filled life. It is in the actual sharing of the Word of God that Jesus becomes real to us and speaks to us. It is in the sharing of the bread that Jesus becomes food for our lives. This is also so when we feed, clothe, and shelter the poor and those who are in need. The actual meeting with a needy person is a potential faith act that verifies the presence of the saving Christ, and it could be a powerful force.

The sacraments, in ritual and ceremonial form, are indeed profoundly sacred acts. The modern Christian believer is encouraged to move beyond outdated thoughts on the sacraments and the other outward signs into an ever more enhancing insight when witnessing our sacred rituals and ceremonies.

10

Dualism: Can the Soul Survive?

As far back as I can remember, I believed there was something very special and eternal about my presence in the world. Created by God, who is immortal, I must possess qualities like God because I have a soul. Furthermore, created by God out of nothing, I felt I was, in some way, eternal. Since I had received this gift of life, all of my Christian education taught me to be good because my immortal soul would be accountable on judgment day. It was not until after I graduated from university that the body/ soul dichotomy (dualism) surfaced as an interesting matter for philosophical debate. Although not philosophically aware of it, most Christians today accept this dichotomy as reality and an essential part of the fabric of belief attached to the clothesline of their faith.

In this chapter, I will focus on the body/soul dichotomy and attempt to show how such a philosophical approach presents challenges as a satisfactory paradigm (way of thinking) about our human nature. Ancient concepts of soul were altered as Hebrew and Greek cultures interacted. In addition, recent research in science has put a physical dimension onto some functions of the brain once thought to be spiritual properties of the soul. These new insights into human nature require us to rethink earlier spiritual concepts about the soul.

When we are treating the body/soul dichotomy, there are considerations that are important to our faith. We tie our soul (immateriality) and life after death (immortality) to our reasons for leading moral lives. We maintain that the just will be rewarded and that there is a just punishment awaiting those who lead immoral lives and cause harm to the innocent and vulnerable. This belief is so entrenched that many Christian churches believe that societal structures would incur severe damage if we were to dismiss a belief in both the existence of a soul and life after death. I am not dismissing these beliefs. What I am saying is that we need to revisit the two ideas: soul and life after death.

Immateriality is different from immortality, and I will treat immortality more fully in the next chapter. The fact that we do think about immateriality and spiritual matters does not automatically necessitate a soul, let alone immortality. Therefore, our discussion will entertain another analogy as a credible alternative. What follows may be disconcerting to those who find comfort in the traditional idea of body and soul being distinct entities. Bear with me, as I believe you will find some ideas thought-provoking.

What Is Soul?

Christian belief maintains that the soul is immaterial in nature. Created out of nothing, it attaches itself to a corporeal substance and relies on matter for full expression. This idea of human nature being one with two entities (body and spirit), as proposed by the church, does not bode well for what science knows about human nature. Furthermore, science struggles with religion's vague perception of what personality means and how our rational nature is not like other animals. The following is an excerpt from the *Catholic Dictionary:*

Soul: the spiritual immortal part in human beings that animates their body. It (soul) is created in respect to the body it will inform, so that the substance of bodily features and of mental characteristics insofar as they depend on organic functions is safeguarded ... a human person is composed of body animated by the soul. In philosophy, animals and plants are also said to have souls, which operate as sensitive and vegetative principles of life. Unlike the human spirit, these souls are perishable. The rational soul contains all the powers of the other souls (animal and vegetative), and is the origin of the sensitive and vegetative functions in the human being.[75]

According to the excerpt above, the Christian understanding of human nature appears to leave little or no room to approach humans' rational presence in the world from an evolutionary point of view. The reason for this is that anything created out of nothing at conception cannot have evolved and cannot be produced by the parents. Furthermore, rationality (a unique aspect of the human soul) can exist outside the body, even after death.

Ancient Platonic and Aristotelian thought, which proposed the existence of forms outside matter and independent of the mind, has fueled the modern Christian idea of the soul. Furthermore, this idea leads one to conclude that not only is the rational dimension immaterial, but it must be immortal as well. The rationality of the human is what separates us from other animals. The rationality (created and infused by God at the time fertilization) is what makes the human being what it is. Finally, it is because of the soul that the body becomes what we call the human body.

I believe a number of these statements to be highly questionable assumptions.

Ancient Understanding of the Soul

Dualism first occurred with Pythagoras as early as the fifth century BCE, was expanded by Aristotle, and finally became concretized by St. Thomas from a religious point of view. The Christian understanding of soul originates in Jewish belief, well after resettlement in Palestine. The traditions of Moses and Abraham did not have our understanding of immateriality and immortality. To live forever was to live in one's progeny, which are to be "numbered as the stars in the heavens."[76] For the ancients, the soul was not a topic for discussion. It is not until the third and fourth centuries BCE that the soul, seen as immaterial with an afterlife, entered into Jewish belief. Some historians maintain that the Platonic and Aristotelian concepts of an independent entity similar to the soul were introduced at this time.

The use of *nepes* (spirit of life) in ancient Hebrew manuscripts will continue to be a matter of debate among scholars. The Hebrews believed the soul was preserved only during life, not after physical death. The spirit of life, the existing life, self, or personhood would be a good description of the ancient understanding. The Sadducees were closer in their beliefs to the ancient Hebrews. They were an influential religious group that did not profess a resurrection of the body into eternal life, as evidenced in the episodes of conflict with Jesus in the gospel narratives.[77]

The introduction of *psyche* (Greek origin) in early Christian thought connotes an enduring quality to the soul, akin to the seat of supernatural life, and resembles the Gnostic thought prevalent during the early formation of the Christian community. The "psyche" is now the object of salvation. Traditional theologians maintain that the Christian idea of soul is a radically new revelation about life and hence salvation. It is my belief that this is more an evolutionary and adaptive conclusion, seeing that there was no second coming and therefore Jesus must indeed become the savior of the soul as well as the world.

The Body of Evidence

No one denies the corporeal nature of the human body. Since the beginning of human history, groups considered the body somewhat special and sacred, as evidenced in the existence of ancient burial sites around the world. However, the admission of reverence for the dead does not necessarily include a belief that after death, the body will unite with the soul to become a glorified body. Such a belief is what most Christians adhere to today. Using our bodies as evidence, we will first examine immateriality and then separate what we mean by immateriality as opposed to immortality.

Immateriality

When speaking of an object as material, we think of a definable substance, quantifiable and lying within the domain of the descriptive laws of science. From this point of view, it is reasonable to say our bodies are objects and exhibit a materiality. Our bodies are material and judged as measureable in many ways. However, an enlightening thing has happened only to humans. After climbing over the evolutionary wall and moving into the upper fringes of the order of primates, we have a distinct recognizable quality about us as members of *Homo sapiens*. The 3–4 percent of genetic material that we do not share with the lower primates results in a radically new organism. We are not only self-sentient, but we self-identify in many ways, have a self-consciousness, and can function, communicate, and predict out and away from the moment at hand. Our innate genetic assembly does not drive all our behavior. We appear to function in such a way as to exhibit more than just a materiality. The church says our souls are not like the souls of other animals. Animal souls perish at death; our souls do not perish at death. The question a scientist has is, how does the church know there is a difference between animal and human souls? I am sure the response is because someone said so, or someone said God revealed this insight. There is really no answer to the question, "Who knows that animal souls do not live forever?" Furthermore, where and when did God reveal this insight?

If I may use an analogy on the physical level, let us say that the function of a fire engine demonstrates an activity that is greater than the sum total of its parts. Looking at a fire engine, the quantifiable mass and energy produce a function beyond the sum total of all the parts, including gas and batteries. The fire engine is a physical phenomenon and is under the control of physical forces explained by the laws of physics. However, we must understand that in our minds, we have put a future purpose to the vehicle so that we expect it to operate as we have intended it to operate, sirens and all.

In the same way, we can speak about the brain. Because the mind is what the brain does (with reservations) in cooperation with the total body, the human being actually exhibits something greater than the sum total of its parts. We exhibit functions that are greater than what comes from our individual parts. Furthermore, as a collective group we exhibit immateriality as our society becomes more complex. It is true that all organisms exhibit a function greater than the sum total of their parts. However, humans are capable of abstracting and accomplishing an infinite number of possibilities with this function, which is different from other animals. My proposition is not a new idea, but as far as I am aware, scholars have not applied it when questioning the theory of dualism.

What I have been proposing to you is the possibility of understanding the human being without being tied down to the body/ soul dichotomy. The traditional Greek analogy, with its way of thinking, does not do justice to what we are learning about the brain and how it functions. The brain is wholly dependent on the body and can never separate itself from the body as it produces an effect that is greater than the sum total of its parts. Hence, I am not speaking at all about a unity of two distinct entities. It is, I admit, very close to understanding human nature as simply "one," not two separate entities of body and soul.

Relating to the quasi-immateriality concept I have brought forward are innumerable instances of mind over matter, but it always requires some bodily interaction for completion. For example, I can trace an imaginary light bulb from my brain to my foot. I use this technique to relieve muscle cramps in my lower body extremities. What is amazing is that, through conceptual construction, a quasi-material light bulb formed in the brain can create a chemical reaction (impulse) resulting in the relaxation of muscular tissue. At present, researchers are not able to pinpoint exactly what and how many neural pathways are involved in such an act, let alone explain how an image of a moving light in the mind can result in muscle relaxation. There is further evidence to support assertions that prior to mind initiating the act, there is a preliminary readiness already in place, involving only a split-second anticipation.[78]

Medical research has shown that the placebo effect often results in the same outcome as the medicinal drug it replaces in clinical trials. Sometimes what we believe will happen actually does happen. We have much to learn about the power of the mind and its capabilities. The human species has just arrived on the evolutionary scene, and the future could be very exciting. As I have mentioned earlier, science has some ideas, but the more it learns, the more there is to learn. I believe that this idea of immateriality will persist for some time. There is something beyond ordinary materiality about the brain, which science needs to address. Will that ever happen? Maybe, but not in our lifetime.

The Frustration of Science with the Theology of the Soul

The church has made innumerable statements on human nature, but every statement finds its basis in ancient philosophical concepts derived from Greek thought. Elaboration of Greek thought resulted in countless proclamations, fabricated on a very static position for everything in nature. Everything is set in place according to the given order of things, revealed by God and transmitted to the believer by the unerring position of the church. Several legitimate complaints arise from this state of affairs.

The first complaint is that the church, with its elaborate fabrications, has taken away a simple appreciation of God and the created soul by trying to explain everything with obtuse concepts and verbiage, resulting in insights that are sterile and devoid of wonder and mystery. If theologians would just let God be a mystery, many issues we are having with religion's focus on the nature of things would not exist. The church's worry today is that science, and what it has to offer, is dancing dangerously close to the areas of knowledge thought to be the domain of religion.

Another complaint is that theologians are always trying to explain religious concepts based on philosophical insights from a pseudo-scientific position that are neither theologically sound nor founded on verifiable data existing in nature. Being unverifiable, such statements on nature cannot be proven or disproven, but under the authority of the church, such pronouncements are not challengeable. In science, there is always an element of mystery. The more that is learned, the more we must learn. Science always follows the evidence. Using an updated vision of the world today, we may ask why modern theology cannot accommodate to some updated vision as well. Theologians since the time of St. Thomas have created a bulk of arguments to fit their preconceived beliefs that are by definition not verifiable. The church expects total acceptance of these beliefs as reality. Concepts on the origin of the soul do not accommodate to the science we now have on human nature.

The third complaint comes from what an educated Christian knows about nature today. There is not a single change in the structure and function of living beings that is not evolutionary. To say that the soul is created out of nothing and then informs a material substance (fertilized egg) is contradictory to what science has proved in its studies of the evolutionary development of humans. *Homo sapiens* shares over 96 percent of its genetic code with other contemporary primates. This means that in the course of evolution, our primitive ancestors have evolved with other primates before the appearance of our species. The church, in theory, is asking us to believe that the remaining 4 percent that is unique to our genetic code is the result of a divine intervention of a miraculous nature (creation from nothing). Furthermore, the created soul informs a fertilized egg with the full attributes of human nature. Once again, this idea of human nature is highly questionable.

Lastly, in protest, we have to say that our personality (defined as soul by some Christian denominations) cannot be entirely immaterial. Our personality is not similar to a ghost living inside us somewhere, only to escape from our body at biological death. Due to serious brain injury, personalities can actually change. In this case, would our souls be changing, as well? A new look at what comprises our being is required. The rest of the matter about immortality lies in the domain of faith, not reason, and does not satisfy the inquiring mind. Remember, immortality is not the domain of science. Science has nothing to say about immortality. However, the advances of science do and will continue to intrude on traditional ideas about human nature.

The Human Dynamo: the New Shift

Let us look at another way of exploring the fact that function indicates something that is greater than the sum total of the parts, even in the world of physics. What we are searching for is a unique way of expressing an identity, not a unity of two entities (i.e., body/soul). We are looking for a better way of expressing an analogy. Recall that the body/soul dichotomy is an analogy, not a reality. Can there be a correlation between function and this new idea of identity? I believe so.

Most people have heard of the word *dynamo*. In applied science, a dynamo refers to an object that is capable of converting mechanical energy into electrical energy by inducing a current of electrons through a metal coil revolving within a magnet. A popular example would be the operation of a hydroelectric dam, which creates electrical energy from water passing over paddles. The paddles force these metal coils to turn inside a magnet, creating a current. An analogy with regard to an energetic person oftentimes depicts him or her as a human dynamo. Let us apply the same term to the soul and also call it a human dynamo.

We first look at the human dynamo as a single entity. The brain, propelled by nutrient and electrochemical stimuli, triggers the products of mental activity, such as insights, emotions, and concepts. In these interactive processes, we have the birth of what we call personality, which continually develops through internal chemistry and external sensory processes. There is no divine intervention activity involved. The associative neurons that generate the cognitive constructs of understanding, memory, and a host of other mental activities culminate in what we call the mind. The mind is much like what the brain does, and we are just beginning to understand the implications of what this means. The analogy of the human dynamo has only one subject (noun), accompanied by a modifier (an adjective). There is only one entity. There is no creation of new functions other than what comes from the dynamo. In faith, we want to believe the mind has an infinite capacity, making it different from any other animal dynamo. Infinite capacity is more a matter of faith at this time, and not a matter of science.

Implications for a Religious Point of View

Having looked at the initial understanding of the words and application of the analogy, what are the implications for the modern Christian believer?

1. The insistence that we are closer to an identity rather than a unity (union of two or more entities) is intriguing. From a spiritual point of view, there would appear to be no room for an entity that outlasts the body.

2. The functional perspective is integral to the dynamo. The dynamo has no meaning and

purpose without being alive. We could say
the same regarding the adjectival portion of
the analogy. We are asked to focus on the
noun portion of the analogy because from the
dynamo comes the beginning of our religious
experiences.

3. The human dynamo produces a function that
    is unique to humans. Not only is the function
    of the entire being greater than the sum total
    of its parts, but its function has an unlimited
    capacity, i.e., beyond any being in evolution-
    ary history. Although function of the dynamo
    flows out of an evolutionary development, it
    has the potential to overcome the restraints
    put upon other organisms. This dynamo pro-
    duces a function that exhibits a unique ca-
    pacity that lifts the present and future above
    the innate drive of lower primates. Using the
    language of science, there is a quasi-infinite
    dimension to the human.[79] This dimension is
    the product of evolution.

Will the Human Dynamo Persist Indefinitely?

One of my college professors told me that the eventual death
rate of human beings is not 100 percent verifiable at any given
time, but rather 99.999 percent. I asked him why this is the case.
His response was that someone could say he has been living
forever. How does one prove him wrong without committing
homicide? Although intended as a comical statement, the instructor knew as well as the students that everyone eventually
dies.

Establishing a new analogy in place of the traditional body/soul dichotomy is important. I chose to separate immortality from immateriality, since the two concepts are not the same. Although the concept of a soul or a spirit-soul was part of an ancient religious belief, a soul possessing enduring qualities came much later. Relating to science, the philosophical conviction that the function of an organism is greater than the sum total of its parts does lie within the domain of the philosophy of science and is an item of inquiry in pursuit of knowledge.

As mentioned at the beginning of this chapter, the topic of the body/soul dichotomy will be a challenge to a devout Christian. It is my belief that, given the inroads of science into religious tenets on the nature of the body, any aspirants to the existence of the soul will have to relinquish some treasured beliefs, or at least look at another paradigm (way of thinking) about the immateriality and immortality of the soul. I have provided the beginning of a new way of understanding human nature for the Christian believer. The human dynamo analogy is credible. However, it is not clear how this discussion will affect one's religious beliefs. Eventually, the modern Christian believer will have to adapt and alter a personal understanding on this matter. The traditional ideas about body/ soul dichotomy (separate entities existing in one nature) will not persist indefinitely. The use of *body and soul* may continue for some time, but we will have to understand them in a different way.

11

Life-after-Death Issues, Where Analogy Abounds

When discussing the body/soul dichotomy in chapter 10, I did not address all issues relating to the soul. What I shared with the reader was the twofold need to structure a new way of talking about the traditional body/soul proposal, as well as distinguishing the soul and its immateriality from a belief in its immortality. While discussing the philosophical theory of dualism, I proposed an alternative analogy, that of the human dynamo. This alternative analogy implies an identity (one entity), not a unity of two entities. The comparison I used is not the reality, only similar to a reality. This way of thinking will permeate what I have to say in this chapter as well.

The following pages will focus on the difficult topic of life after death. I am not here to propose another life-after-death scenario. Furthermore, as a Christian I do not attempt to deny a future eternal life. What I am saying is that, just as we examined traditional concepts of soul with a new analogy, we also need to look at what we mean by life after death. Most people dislike talking about death, let alone what happens after death. Death is certain. No one knows for sure if there is a life after death, let alone what kind of afterlife it might be.

Faith in Life after Death

What do Christians rely on at this point? We have a theological virtue that we call faith. Faith is a personal conviction that something is true or will happen. All religions preach beliefs that assert a spiritual reality of some kind, which is part of a faith experience. This is not just a judgment arising from the minds of the uneducated, but expressed also by educated individuals as well.

Many scientists today believe in God. They believe in the existence of a soul made eternal by the redeeming works of Christ. We could say the same about people of other religions that hold immortality as an important item of faith. Reasons for belief in immortality may differ greatly but are valued nonetheless. I have a friend who is both scientist and a Muslim, whom I asked about life after death. His answer was that he did not want to know; it would break the suspense.

We know that faith is not solely a religious function. Upon entering a room, we exhibit a form of faith in expecting that the lights will turn on when we flip the switch. We expect and believe that the lights will turn on so we can see. As a theological virtue, faith also operates from a set of convictions inherent in the believer so we can discover something more about ourselves. An act of faith bridges the gap between our quasi-immateriality and our supposed immortality. Such a thought is not within the domain of science but is a discovery that comes from within the human dynamo. We must remember that science cannot prove or disprove any belief in immortality. Science is dependent on physical proof and verifiability.

One's faith does not need to have physical evidence, because it has accepted an authority and has placed trust in that authority (Christ). As such, this mind-set needs no physical proof. If matters of faith were evident, our faith would cease. Christ did die (no physical doubt about it), but also Christ rose from the dead (a matter of faith, not science). Consequently, the accomplishment of the Savior put an eternal meaning to our faith. Since science has little to say about immortality, our faith in an afterlife will always involve faith in someone's word (the good news of Christ) and a strong hope. Horace, the Roman, poet proclaimed, "Non omnis moriar."[80] By this, he meant his influence would not altogether pass away, but would live on in his works. Being an admitted atheistic hedonist, he believed and hoped in something, but it was not a religious hope.

In Holy Scripture, the treatment of the body and soul illustrates an extremely rich tradition and ever-changing understanding about an eternal spirit embodied in men and women. The concepts of immortality of the soul and life after death came rather late in the Jewish religion, and many members of the Jewish belief do not accept the concept even to this day. Even among Christians, there is a hesitancy to discuss what lies ahead for the dying person, and people today would rather think and talk about an earthly form of heavenly life as preached by the early church. Remember Jesus did not return as had been expected. Accordingly, thoughts had to refocus on what would happen when Jesus comes to save the just, or when we die. It is true, when using common terms such as *life* and *death*, that major starting points will not be the same. *Life* and *death* are like *love* and *goodness*. They are terms that few define in the same way and upon which everyone has an opinion that could carry an element of credibility. I would like to use the ideas of a well-known priest biologist to explain eternal fulfillment that would be a form of analogy of life after death.

A Visionary with a Futuristic Analogy

Teillard de Chardin, SJ (1881–1955), in his best-known work, *The Phenomenon of Man*, wrote about the movement of nature from an alpha position to an omega point. In his mystical way, Chardin provided us with a directional sense as we observe nature becoming ever more complex. This process will lead humankind forward to total fulfillment. To explain this purposeful evolutionary movement, he assigned a new meaning to the late nineteenth century term *orthogenesis*. In Chardin's understanding, creation is fashioning its living entities toward producing the pinnacle of beings, and that would be humankind. Humanity directs itself to an endpoint, at which time it will find fulfillment in the omega, the endpoint and purpose of creation from its very beginning. From his theological perspective, the omega point is God.

As one would expect, Chardin's work caused both negative and positive reaction around the world. Both the religious conservatives and biologists criticized his ideas. Changing the act of creation from a static event to an evolutionary process was not acceptable to the Roman Catholic Church and other Christian denominations. In turn, the biological theorists of the day took issue with any purposeful direction embedded in living organisms, especially since survival of the fittest depended upon random changes in the gene pool. In addition, *Homo sapiens* exists only because of the adaptive nature of the human body and, with its large endocranial capacity, has become the dominant species on earth.

Fr. Chardin, no doubt, was a very holy priest-paleontologist, who sincerely believed that the creative power of God penetrated nature in every aspect and that humankind is to envelop itself, at some point, into the very likeness of God the creator. The evolutionary process described in his works was more than Darwinian natural selection, since his work led to a unified spiritual thinking on the matter. His writings were both mystical and potent, and they attempted to explain how he believed God works in nature. Such insights may be somewhat passé today, but his influence on spiritual matters will never be forgotten. From what I understand, Chardin's use of "omega point" referred to the species endpoint rather than to personal fulfillment for each of us after death. However, in his mystical books and writings, he references humans as being cells enveloped (at the end of time) into the cosmic Christ and says that in heaven, we will be contemplating God as through the eyes of Christ.[81] Though somewhat vague, these ideas open up new ways of thinking about eternity. Before we propose a new analogy for life after death, it would be beneficial to see how science uses analogy as a research tool in describing new ideas and discoveries.

Use of Analogy in Science

Georges Lamaitre (1894–1966), a priest, an amazing mathematical genius and compatriot of Einstein, first explained the origin of the universe. Lamaitre compared the origin of the universe first to a development from a "cosmic egg." This egg resembled a concentration of all matter to a single quantum.[82] The analogy (some might prefer to call it a metaphor) was not taken seriously, as it represented a novel theory among theoretical physicists of the day. Frederick Hoyle comically ridiculed Lamaitre's proposal as nothing more than a "big bang."[83] This term subsequently went viral and is used as a powerful analogy today. Unfortunately, astronomers consider the big bang more a reality than just a description of something we can only surmise to have happened. What they speak of may turn out to be correct. However, at present, we cannot validate the big bang outside a complex set of mathematical calculations derived from a set of complicated instrumental data. Treatment of the big bang theory as an analogy does not invalidate it as a genuine scientific comparison. It is something upon which one can further research and develop new ideas. A case in point would be Stephen Hawking's use of the term *singularity*, which proposes the idea of the presence of only energy resulting in a big bang.[84] In this analogy, there is little or no matter, only an incomprehensible surge of energy.[85] The point is, if there is a place for analogy (concerning the origin of the universe) in a world of verifiable science, and while such theories are not entirely verifiable, certainly there should be a place for the use of analogy in the world of religion and an act of faith.

Analogy Applied to *Homo Sapiens* and Darwinism

When one considers the evolution of species, history appears to be "written" with beginnings. We know, as biologists, that something happened when we discover the presence of new species, and we presume some archetype[86] has given birth to a novelty. We presume the archetypal figure disappeared only because there is no evidence of its presence later on, as recorded by scientific research. In traditional biology, the appearance of a new species (beginning) occurs because of a total random process, with the species's ability to use these random changes to its benefit. When external changes occur in the environment, a species may or may not become or remain successful. We can say there are no purposeful changes or direction involved in the discussion of new beginnings for life forms (Darwin's premise). However, now that *Homo sapiens* has entered into the picture with its ability to control life forms (as opposed to only random changes occurring), perhaps some accommodations need to be made about Darwin's initial premise. Let me explain what I mean by the need for a change of thought here.

It is my conviction that humankind is the only life form that actually exhibits the ability to control not just its own direction in evolution, but the evolution and direction of other life forms. The natural development of human endocranial capacity and its neural organization are putting us on the verge of altering and controlling other life forms, for weal or woe (new beginnings for nature). While many philosophers and empirical scientists have talked about an unlimited capacity of the mind and how humankind has no limits to what it can achieve, these statements could be just suppositions of the mind. However, it seems that is exactly what is happening today and probably will be happening more in the future. The question is, when will such a supposition become a fact? It is likely just a matter of time. I am not considering the social and economic dimensions at this point, but only the biological parameters of human existence.

Beginnings take on a new meaning in Darwinian evolution, when a species can alter its genetic and/or congenital structures, independent of random changes in the genetic code. This process is relatively free of external pressures forcing adaptive measures for survival. At present, millions upon millions of individuals are surviving and living long lives when in the ordinary course of events they would never have made it to maturity or contributed offspring into the gene pool. It is insightful to think this is just the beginning of *Homo sapiens's* influence in the world today. Truly, humankind is constantly being ushered into new beginnings in the world of science and technology. What I believe we are leading up to is that beginnings, not endings, is the best way to explain what lies ahead for us. The reader can detect a bit of Chardin's thought on this matter However, this is just another way of comparing ideas.

New Beginnings Applied to a Personal Life after Death

St Paul spoke very eloquently about matters relating to the second coming of Christ, life after death, and eternal life in Christ. One would not expect Paul to take much time elaborating on something of which he could not be certain. What he said is that, although personal death is a reality, so is eternal life a reality (of faith) through the resurrection of Christ. His assumption is truly an assumption by way of analogy. Reading Paul correctly will lead one to understand that his vision of the afterlife was a matter of faith and not a validation of fact. If the resurrection were a verifiable fact, then there would be no need for faith, no salvation by faith, according to Paul. The problem arises when he preaches about spiritual death and physical death in the same breath and connotation, as he does in chapter 6 of his letter to the Romans. It is very easy to fall into the false assumption that our life after death is a verifiable reality and not a matter of faith.

We need to remember that the scientific method and demonstrable science we take for granted today were not in Paul's life. He spoke innumerable times about spiritual death, new life in Christ, and a new life starting with the acceptance of Jesus as savior. However, the early disciples expanded the new life, which Jesus brought to the disciples, into a vision of the future as a resurrection of the body. This is so because the kingdom of God did not come as the disciples had expected. What was once understood as the analogy Jesus used, about the new life of the Father's kingdom on earth residing in one's heart, has now become some sort of glorified life for the early Christians. This would be similar to the life talked about in the postresurrection narratives. The problem is that from the early days of the church, theologians applied this idea of new life in Christ here on earth to what happens after physical death. This, I believe, represents a definite change in beliefs about an afterlife.

This discussion about redoing our traditional approach to life after death could be disturbing and somewhat shocking for some. It is not that I am asking anyone to forego traditional thoughts on what the afterlife might be, but to look at this matter of faith in a different manner. If traditional beliefs work for you, hang on to them. However, for many inquirers, traditional beliefs do not work. Let us now discuss another way of looking at life after death.

Beginnings, Not Endings

One fascinating aspect of Jesus's teaching, whether in the form of parable, metaphor, or analogy, is that Jesus emphasizes the purpose of the incident. Nearly all episodes relating to the nature of the kingdom of heaven (parable of the prodigal son, the lost coin, and innumerable other stories) focus on a new life, a new beginning, as it were. Even in accounts of cures performed by Jesus, the direction He was proposing was that of entering into a new life. On the cross, the words Jesus had for the man hanging next to Him were about being with Him that day in paradise, not dying or being dead with Him. Physical death is a reality. We know nothing about the other side of life, only an unfathomable promise of something new, different, and unexplainable.

We can only speak analogically about another form of life, unlike what we know as physical life. In this "new beginning," the analogy is not a physical life after death. There is in faith only a beginning of a new experience. The following are some summary examples of faith items relating to death and life after death that we need to reshape. I support these comments by conclusions reached in earlier chapters in this book.

1. **Death:** The issue is about spiritual death as opposed to physical death. Jesus was preaching about spiritual death of the soul, which prevents one from living the kingdom of the

Father here on earth. This kingdom was not physical or full of individuals who had glorified bodies. The kingdom resides in a believer's heart, which at present has a definite life span. Yes, the kingdom of God is now alive and on earth. The new life Jesus preached about is not life after death, but the life of a person who lives the good news of the Father on earth. Jesus used stories familiar to the people of His time, but through analogy and metaphor, He preached a novel and unfamiliar idea. The kingdom of His Father was His antithesis to spiritual death, not physical death. It is our faith that keeps an eternal kingdom alive today. Without the kingdom of the Father in our hearts, there is death. I am not denying a life after death. I am saying that our faith in the kingdom of God on earth invites us to think about our call to be Christians, and that is the only thing as Christians that really matters, not death.

2. **Life after death:** When the end of the world (eschaton) did not come as the early Christians had expected, the believers thought out the matter of eternity in different ways that strayed away from the teachings in Jesus's parables. It is important to remember that the Old Testament writers did not think of another life after death, or at least another life that went on forever. A soul living forever was not in their vocabulary. Immortality consisted in one's lineage enduring forever.

Although Jesus's idea of His Father's kingdom on earth was a novel idea, I believe that Hellenistic thought also influenced early Christian thinking. This does not mean that there is not an afterlife. What happens after death is a matter of faith. We simply do not know anything about a life after death.

3. **The eternal soul:** If one is speaking about the spiritual dimensions of *Homo sapiens's* body, then religious tenets must accommodate the data from scientific research that indicates functions of the brain taking over much of what we call soul. The power of mind, as it functions, is not altogether about something spiritual but is necessarily connected with neural-electrical and biochemically based processes as well. Scientists simply do not know all that there is to know about such processes, only that there is a correlation between what happens electrochemically in the brain and what the mind does. The mind is not the soul and is not eternal. Neither is the human condition or human nature eternal, contrary to the traditional understanding of soul.

    The reader must be careful at this point. Science is not capable of reducing a traditional spirit or soul theory to material functions. The mind is what the brain does, but it is not a simple cause-and-effect relationship. Furthermore, if one thinks the spirit or soul is created at the time of the union of a sperm and egg, such a belief verges on the incredible, when all other life forms exhibit their own somewhat less sophisticated spirit and soul. It is possible that what we call eternal soul is really an evolutionary development of an extraordinary power within the brain. This conjecture does not dispel the soul's eternal nature. This power is the property of *Homo sapiens,* and no other organism exhibits this power and potential. You can think of it as inner power on a journey that never ends—that is to say, always a new beginning. Call this power anything you wish—a soul, perhaps. I choose to call it a human dynamo.

4. **The glorified and resurrected body:** It is important to recall the earlier discussions on the changes that have taken place in Holy Scripture after Jesus left the presence of the disciples. Postresurrection narratives exhibit numerous redactions. It is like changes in the vocal transmission between hundreds of listeners, each of whom claims his or her understanding was the correct wording and the way things happened. Most Christians today maintain that a glorified body means a state like Jesus's body at the time of His transfiguration or ascension. However, the doubting Thomas looking at the pierced hands, St. Peter experiencing Jesus as the man cooking fish over a fire on the beach, and the disciples meeting the man on the road to Emmaus have a much different connotation and not

a sense of any glorified body. These are all postresurrection experiences that the apostles experienced as corporeal thinkers, imagining flesh components, not glorified or resurrected components. If the sensation experience took place, it would be material and measurable, not a glorified ghost. The apostles understood their contact with Jesus as a measurable experience. If this experience of the apostles actually happened, it was not an experience of a glorified and resurrected body of Christ. A glorified and resurrected body is not credible enough for me, a man of faith, to keep it hanging on my clothesline of faith.

The teachings of Paul are a critical point in this discussion. If Christ did not rise from the dead, our certainty of faith in our own immortality and in our own resurrected bodies is in vain.[87] The deposit of faith (not fact) held the early community together, and these essential doctrines evolved into what we hold dear today. I have introduced a different starting point that could move this discussion further. It is not an answer but a direction.

Conclusion

We have discussed in this chapter the need to revisit certain doctrines or beliefs that originated from questionable positions taken by the early Christian communities. These beliefs became entrenched and set in stone by those early thinkers greatly influenced by Greek thoughts on the material versus the immaterial. What the early fathers of the church picked up from Greek thought became solemn and workable statements on the mortality of the body versus the eternal nature of the soul. Very little movement has taken place to resolve this dualistic dilemma for the believer. I believe we need to replace the body/soul dichotomy and fall in line with some analogy that accommodates to our changing ideas of human nature. We need to work with a faith in "new beginnings," rather than struggle with an idea of where we will go after the ending—that is, death.

12

The Certainty of Faith and Science

There are many works published which treat issues in science and religion. Some of these works have attempted to show there are no real conflicts between what science demonstrates and what religion teaches. Such a position maintains that as long as science stays focused on the measurable and religion preaches on matters of an eternal and spiritual nature, there should be no quarrels. However, such an expectation is rarely realized. Human nature does not operate with two such disciplines always isolated, and with insulated perspectives that never make contact. Overlapping does occur in the fields of medicine, bioethics, and principles of moral behavior. Conflicts do arise from a religious perspective because of a vested interest in a literal interpretation of the Bible: God speaks and the issue is final. For conservative believers, there is only one cosmology: the cosmology of the ancients. On the other hand, science has no interest in the cosmology of the ancients. Religious matters lie outside the domain of science. What is at the source of a conflict between science and religion? It is the scientist and the fundamentalist having issues. However, it is true that opinions from scientists oftentimes stir the troubling waters of most conflicts. Scientists are adept at rooting up contradictions and exposing irrational assumptions.

With a novel approach, I will attempt to sort out what I believe to be the domain of science from the domain of religion. The method by which I hope to achieve this objective is by clarifying ideas about certainty. I choose to call these ideas the certainty of faith in religion and the certainty of fact in science. An answer to the question of domain of these two disciplines lies in establishing what one means by being certain.

Throughout all my chapters, I have attempted to show the reader the importance of sifting out less worthy components of a faith experience while preserving treasured beliefs passed on from a rich religious tradition. At the same time, I have insisted that any beliefs contrary to what has been demonstrated by science need to change and evolve. It is true that some scientific theories about the origin of the universe may appear somewhat conjectural, but only because some theories involve analogy as a starting point for discussion. In earlier chapters, I showed that we use analogy in both science and religion, with the intention of explaining some things that lie somewhat outside our grasp. To resolve this impasse for the modern Christian believer, we will need to look deeper into the source of our own religious convictions.

It is important to understand the extent to which people on each side of the question have moved into areas not clearly defined. Both scientists and religious conservatives have fallen short in clearly defining their terms of reference. In Christian tradition, from which we have derived the content of beliefs for our faith line, there was originally no other side to the question. Since science was not available to the early Christians, all matters pertaining to the validity of religious belief about God and nature surfaced in a religious doctrine of some kind.

Looking at our faith line is not the same as looking at something material and measureable. For instance, life after death is a conviction arising from faith and hope. The very presence of this conviction must necessarily involve doubt, as well. Like love, hate, and beauty, faith is a quality of a spiritual nature and lacks a physical measuring stick. If a scientist enters the discussion with the intent of disproving religious faith, it would be an incorrect and unscientific attempt. Since faith is outside the domain of science, any discussion by a scientist about matters relating to this type of religious faith could only be hypothetical and conjectural.

The Certainty of Faith

We will open this discussion on certainty of faith with a focus on what is happening when religious reaction to matters of the origin of the universe and of *Homo sapiens* surfaces. In past works by agnostic and atheistic philosopher-scientists, as well as religious fundamentalists, we have clear examples of an impasse with regard to science and religion. Both moderate and conservative religious leaders have continually confronted scientific theory with the conviction that there really is no absolute scientific proof of anything. Such a complaint may have some validity. However, I maintain that this thinking carries a bias toward preserving ancient traditional belief, over and above what a third party or an arm's-length observer would accept as true. A conflict of interest in favor of adherence to biblical beliefs prevents an honest discussion. Using the Bible as a resource manual or fact book that monitors and directs discoveries in science does damage to lasting values found in sacred manuscripts. Scientific propositions put forward become a threat to this biased stance, resulting in a protective attitude. This is unfortunate because such an approach vitiates a key point in what it means to be certain in a faith experience.

The certainty of faith, although possessing many qualities of being real, has no business intruding into the domain of scientific investigation and verifiable facts. We can never attempt to use doctrinal statements as measuring sticks. We can dictate the object of faith to be real, but this dictate cannot be demonstrated. As a Christian, I believe there resides in our minds and hearts an internal admission of some kind of deity's existence. This admission goes well beyond any doctrinal pronouncement. To deny this is to go against the power of the mind that searches for a fulfilment (God) with its faith line. For example, individual beliefs and proclamations can come and go, but faith in the good news of Jesus or any other religious figure in history will last forever because faith comes with the entire human condition, not just the cognitive components.

Let us look further into what we sometimes think is a certainty of faith. The certainty of faith is not like a proof for the existence of a deity. This certainty does not persist because of a set of arguments based on an insight into nature or from the rational thinking of the mind. Since the time of the early Greeks, propositions have come forward attempting to convince inquirers of the validity of an argument. For example, from the time of Plato, philosophical tenets convinced the intellectually elite that God must exist. St Augustine preached that the existence of the idea of truth affirms the existence of the cause of all truth. Any truth assumes an unquestionable (indubitable) truth, and it is God.

Other examples of intellectual conviction from philosophy would be the following:

1. **Exemplarism** was one of the first ideas that connected God to the ideal form existing outside the mind.

2. **Emanation** was an argument that all matter flows forth as part of a divine quality (somewhat similar to pantheism) that desires perfection, and that perfection is God.

3. **Prime mover** arises from rationalizing to the source and creator of all things coming into existence.

4. **Causality,** which is an argument from an effect to a final cause, is a popular proof subscribed to even in modern times.

5. **Intelligent design,** quite popular among the fundamentalists, concerns itself with the conviction that nature could not have achieved such perfection (e.g., the human eye) without there being a creator.

All of the above philosophical propositions for certainty of a God in an act of faith fall short on the logic of the arguments.[88] The reasoning process in all of these propositions is flawed. Although my reasons for saying this might be interesting for some, an explanation would be lengthy and distracting at this point. I am asking the reader to assume that there is no certain proof for the existence of God and that we must look elsewhere for an understanding of our certainty of faith. Faith in a religious entity or religious value carries with it real certainty, though a certainty not physically verifiable and not always intellectually convincing. It is important to realize that our certainty of faith must continually be developing (evolving). The advances and discoveries of science should support our faith experience and not diminish its importance. Our faith should progress

from within the entire framework of the human condition—
that is, the entire human dynamo.

We can intellectually think that the concept of God is a construct
of the mind, but at no time can we imply that this construct is all
and the only value to the God experience. As we move forward in
the experience of God and some items of belief change or take on
new meaning, we will discover more of what our God means for
us. Remember, God is present in this human journey, and with
the advances of science, our faith in Him should become an even
more enlightening experience. The discovery of what God could
mean propels us forward, as if in pursuit of something beyond our
comprehension. Like the other two virtues of hope and charity,
the certainty of faith issues forth in an ever deeper conviction that
God is an ongoing discovery through a journey forward into the
unknown. This journey fills us with expectation (hope) of something always beyond the grasp of complete understanding. This
experience is our certainty of faith. This experience is as real as
the air we breathe yet cannot see.

The Certainty of Fact

When discussing the domain of science, I have considered discoveries as factual. In all the chapters, I have maintained the
necessity for the key criterion of verifiability. Certainty enters in
as a conviction that what the scientists can prove by some kind
of measuring stick must indeed be correct. I say correct, but not
correct absolutely, since science always functions within certain
restrictive parameters. A scientist must demonstrate in the physical sense his or her discovery for all to substantiate. Science, which
bears the scrutiny of peer reviews and documentation, exists in
a fundamentally different world of research from any other type
of discipline. Being able to produce results from an acceptable

chest of measuring instruments is always the objective. Not only do scientists investigate the accumulated data, but they also predict for purposes of moving research into new areas of potential discoveries.

The idea of theory in modern science is much more than an assumption or an idea. Theories like the theory of evolution and the theory of molecular similarities found in the science of molecular biology are only theories in the methodological sense, much like working hypotheses, and not like the traditional understanding of theory at the time of Darwin. When using certainty in the area of science, one always assumes the discovery must stay within the parameters of a given hypothesis. By this I mean a researcher concludes that the work done is valid, as long as all the perceived variables have been covered and accounted for under laboratory conditions. For the reader's information, variables are the unknown and known factors that could alter a hypothesis. In addition, science can declare research as valid until, or even when, it is subsumed by a larger encompassing theory.

Science can also deal with negative outcomes and certainties. It is possible to reach factual certainty when declaring a preexisting hypothesis to be not probable. This is very common in physical sciences and offers great insight and direction for further research. Within the areas of medicine and nutrition, it is particularly common to find such type of research occurring. Scientists continually question areas of research and have to reorient their convictions due to the surfacing of unknown variables. This type of certainty is fine and good, since it always leads us to further insight into the wonders of nature.

We are at a point in our discussion of certainty in science where challenges appear. Many scientists in theoretical physics fall victim to a fallacy that just because they cannot verify a religious tenet scientifically, their own view of reality must be the correct one. Such thinking usually leads individuals out of the domain of science into the domain of religion. Nikita Khrushchev's false attribution to the first Russian cosmonaut that "there is no God out there" is very characteristic of the antireligious propaganda at the time.[89] Yuri Gargarin (the first cosmonaut) actually said no such thing.

Richard Dawkins, a notable scientist in his own field, professes atheism and openly says as much when questioned about a point of view on religion. He is quoted as saying, "I am against religion because it teaches us to be satisfied with not understanding the world" and "One of the things that is wrong with religion is that it teaches us to be satisfied with answers which are not really answers at all."[90] What is interesting here, possibly unbeknownst to him, is that he is slipping into the same error that Nikita Khrushchev did. There is more to understanding the world than just what science brings to the table. Again, it would be as if I said we cannot prove the existence of God, and therefore there is no God. Ironically, as some of the critics in his own field have mentioned, Dawkins, a diehard atheist, is putting up his own position to be a form of religion. I say this because he may have slipped into a certainty that is not physically verifiable—that is, insisting there is no God.

We need to ask ourselves whether all certainties that we experience are reducible to the measuring sticks of science. It is my belief that scientists fall short when attempting to measure areas of moral, artistic, and religious enrichment in society with the tools of science. Furthermore, one can describe and analyze various achievements and events occurring in society, but no one can predict them accurately. Oftentimes, there may be too many variables coming into question that inhibit any reliable scientific approach. Finally, science achieves certainty of fact by a form of measurement, but this process always carries with it the possibility of having to face new challenges when a more accurate measuring stick is used. This is what we mean by certainty of fact in science.

I am convinced that the ongoing tension between the discoveries of science and the certainty of faith is a healthy situation for the modern Christian because it forces each side of the discussion to work within its own domain and to figure out what that domain might be. As we move into the future, we should always look forward to a closer relationship between science and religion. The concept of what is real should be valid for all to enjoy. This allows all to move ahead into a future that incorporates the values of science into the basic drive men and women have to be a people of faith.

The Final Word

The evolution of belief as treated in this work comprises just a snapshot of the growth and development of Christianity over the centuries of its existence. In summary, I will make the following comments.

One can witness two major phenomena, growing out of Jewish thought and the influence of Hellenistic philosophy, occurring: adaptation and accommodation. These religious changes had to occur for the survival of the Christian tradition. Initial adaptation and accommodation surfaced as an attempt to solve some misunderstandings about both the second coming of Jesus and the nature of Christ. When the move of the ruling church to Rome took place (fourth century), there were serious and oftentimes violent challenges with the early heresies in Asia Minor. We should not forget the major schisms that resulted in adaptive responses within the mainline church. I speak of the Eastern Church (eleventh century), Henry VIII (sixteenth century) and the consequent birth of the Church of England, and lastly the Reformation (sixteenth century) brought on by Martin Luther.

The time of the Holy Roman Empire (tenth to nineteenth centuries) and the Roman Catholic Church (eleventh century to present), which dominated the Renaissance into modern times, was fraught with challenges brought on by the warring kingdoms. In the Roman Catholic Church, corruption and the loss of a sense of spiritual purpose resulted in elaborate institutional structures needed for survival. In the attempt to establish a false sense of control and the status quo in religious beliefs, inquisitional practices became widespread in most parts of Europe.

With the onset of the industrial revolution (eighteenth and nineteenth centuries), we had Christian churches attempting to survive within a growing rationalistic, libertarian philosophy and apathy toward anything religious. Christian churches have had to adapt and accommodate or become irrelevant. With the far-reaching influence of science today, this is even more the case for the survival of Christianity.

From an evolutionary point of view, there is good reason to be optimistic for religious belief. As society has become more complex, and with the education of masses, there is a gradual movement away from irrational and unverifiable proclamations into an internal form of inward discovery of God. As mentioned several times in this work, humankind has been on earth a very short time. We are just beginning to understand what a religious experience is and what experience of God can mean for us. In the evolution of belief, the part played by a dominant religious leadership was extremely important because that form of leadership educated the masses; that form of leadership held together the fabric of values we needed to develop into the sophisticated societies and worshipping communities of today. However, traditional Christianity needs to take a different perspective for the future. We need to move on from the irrelevant edicts, doctrines, and infallible proclamations originating from biblical authority and divest ourselves of some personal convictions. The teachings of the early fathers of the church are important now, but more as lessons of history than static dictates.

No one can predict the future of Christian belief. Know for sure that as our faith continues, the drive for a discovery of what God means here and now will require a constant pursuit of a fulfillment beyond our grasp. The kingdom of heaven is already in our believing hearts. An internal acceptance of the kingdom is all that matters. What lies ahead is what we are always searching for, but it should not be something that causes worry. The kingdom of God is already present. What lies ahead is just another new beginning.

Endnotes

Introduction

1   The use of this phrase is adapted from a novel by Yann Martel, *The High Mountains of Portugal* (Toronto: Alfred A. Knopf Canada, 2016). The original quote on page 131 of the book is "We are risen apes, not fallen angels." I altered this phrase because of the following inaccuracy: both apes and *Homo sapiens* have in common an archetype (ancestor), which would necessarily be a primate, not an ape.

Chapter 1

2   The reader may wish to follow the controversy involved in the interpretation of St. Paul's Letter to the Romans (5:12) with the use of "because all men have sinned," in place of "in whom all men have sinned." There is truly no satisfactory resolution to this conflicting interpretation. The reader may consult two sources: John L. McKenzie, *Dictionary of Theology* (Milwaukee: Bruce Publishing Company, 1965), 820; or Karl Rahner and Herbert Vorgrimler, *Theological Dictionary*, 329–30. Both sources fail the test of the verifiable evolutionary origin of humankind, and rather concentrate on false theological assumptions.

3   McKenzie, *Dictionary of the Bible*, 858. An original source of the existence of the synoptic gospels (Q, German *Quelle*) is a constant matter of controversy, depending on which allegiance one holds: non-Catholic or Catholic source of scholarship.

4   A good reference for further research would be *Encyclopedia Britannica: Macropedia*, 15th ed., s.v. "Bibilical literature."

Chapter 2

5   Acts of the Apostles 5:1–11.

6   For a good history of Jerusalem, consult *Encyclopedia Britannica: Macropedia*, 15th ed., s.v. "Jerusalem."

7   *Encyclopedia Britannica: Macropedia*, 15th ed., s.v. "Jesus Christ."

Chapter 3

8   *Encyclopedia Britannica: Macropedia*, s.v. "Production of Simple Organic Molecules."

9   Ibid, s.v. "Polymers."

10   Courtney Humphries, "Life's Beginnings," *Harvard Magazine*, September, 2013.

11   Arthur Kornberg, "A Lifelong Love Affair with Enzymes," *Scientist*, September 4, 1989.

Chapter 4

12   Genesis 2: 5.

13   Mckenzie, *Dictionary of the Bible*, 158–159.

14   Walter Isaacson, *Einstein* (New York: Simon and Schuster, 2007), 335. Written by Einstein to Max Born on December 4, 1926.

15   Dan Talpalariu, "Pope Benedict Meets Stephen Hawking: The Pontiff Agrees to Empirical Science as an Act of God," *Softpedia News*, November 3, 2008, http://www.news.softpedia.com/new/Pope-Benedict-Meets-Stephen-Hawking.

16 See note 2 above; italics added.

17 See note 1 above.

18 Genesis 22:17, 26:4. The quote shows how immortality is understood by the Hebrews.

19 John 18:36.

Chapter 5

20 Bart Ehrman, *Misquoting Jesus* (San Francisco: Harper, 2005), 72, 124.

21 Ibid., 149.

22 Ibid., 159.

23 John 1:12; Romans 8:14; 2 Corinthians 6:18.

24 Ehrman, *Misquoting Jesus*, 152–162.

25 Ibid., 167.

26 Ibid., 165–170.

27 Ibid., 157.

Chapter 6

28 *Funk and Wagnalls Standard Dictionary: International Edition,* s.v. "conscience."

29 Ibid., s.v. "prescriptive," definition 5.

30 *Encyclopedia Brittanica: Micropedia*, 15th ed., s.v. "natural law." Also, *Brittanica Macropedia*, s.v. "natural law."

31 *Funk and Wagnalls Standard Disctionary*, s.v. "descriptive," definition 3.

32 "Church Teaching on In Vitro Fertilization," *The Catholic World Report*, November 29, 2012.

33 Rev. Kevin McGovern, director of the Centre for Health Ethics in Melbourne, Australia.

Chapter 7

34 MacKenzie, *Dictionary of the Bible*, 774–775.

35 Ibid., 317.

36 Luke 10:18. Mackenzie, *Dictionary of the Bible*, 775, states, "This obscure saying is not to be taken as reference to the preexistence of Jesus nor as an affirmation of the Jewish story of the fall of the angels, but as an allusion to the pride which goes before a fall."

37 Karl Rahner and Herbert Vorgrimler, *Theological Dictionary* (New York: Herder and Herder, 1968), 20–22, 156–157.

38 Job 1:6 ff, 2:1 ff.

39 McKenzie, *Dictionary of the Bible*, 878–879.

40 Ibid., 879.

41 *The Catholic Encyclopedia* (New York: Appleton Company, 1909), as reviewed by the *New Advent*, points out the initiation of these orders as separate from ordination during Pope Fabian's reign (236–251 CE). When applied to minor exorcisms, as found in baptismal ceremonies

today, the reference is *Manuel of Minor Exorcism* by Julius Porteous (London: Catholic Truth Society, 2012), 210–234.

42 Yasmine Hafiz, "Exorcism Conference at Vatican," *Huffington Post*, May 13, 2014. Also, Barbie Latza Nadeau, "Pope Francis gives Blessing to Exorcist Conference," *Daily Beast*, October 29, 2014.

43 Roy F. Baumeister and John Tierney, *Will Power: Rediscovering the Greatest Human Strength* (New York: Penguin Press, 2011).

Chapter 8

44 The Dalai Lama, *The Universe in a Single Atom: The Convergence of Science and Spirituality* (New York: Morgan Road Books, 2005), 24–25. The actual quote is "If scientific analysis were to conclusively demonstrate certain claims in Buddhism to be false, then we must accept the findings of science and abandon those claims."

45 *Encyclopedia Britannica: Macropedia*, s.v. "the homunculus theory."

46 The matter of therapeutic abortion illustrates at least a partial turn-around of the Magisterium, as medical science becomes clear on the matter. The "Pope Pius XI Encyclical," taken from *The Papal Encyclicals in their Historical Context*, ed. Anne Fremantle (The New American Library, 1956), 241, states specifically the illicit nature of therapeutic abortions. However, Pope Paul VI, "On the Regulation of Birth," (St. Paul Edition, 1968), 12, discusses the "Licitness of Therapeutic Means." In summary, the intention to save the mother, and still not to intend to kill the fetus in the process, is convoluted at best. The only way to save the mother is to participate actively in the baby's death. One is deliberately causing the death of the unborn in examples like ectopic pregnancies, even though doctors may not like the idea.

47 St. Thomas, *On the Sentences, 4:31.2.2 Reply to ob.4*. At this point St. Thomas implies that masturbation, coitus interruptus and spilling seed are worse than rape because they involve an injury to God, whereas laws that issue from man (reason), e.g., rape, are not a violation of laws

of nature (what we call natural law), which issue forth from God. For further information, see Aline H. Kalbian, *Sex, Violence, and Justice: Contraception and the Catholic Church* (Washington, DC: Georgetown University Press, 2014).

48 Mark 10:1–9.

49 http://www.aggiecatholicblog.org/2015/is-premarital-sex -always-wrong/.

50 *Merriam Webster Dictionary*, s.v. "paranormal." *Paranormal* is understood as a not scientifically explainable phenomenon. First known use was 1905.

51 Ibid., s.v. "supernatural." *Supernatural* is understood as that which is beyond nature. First known use was in the fifteenth century.

52 Ted Slowick, "Pope Francis Calls for Compassion for Gay People," *Chicago Tribune*, June 28, 2016. Several quotes from Pope Francis on the need to show compassion for gays.

53 Robin Marantz Henig, "Rethinking Gender," *National Geographic*, January 2017, 51.

54 Epigenetics is defined as the study of the way in which the expression of heritable traits is modified by environmental influences or other mechanisms without a change to the DNA sequence. First coined by C. H. Waddington, British biologist (1905–1975).

55 Henig, "Rethinking Gender." This reference relates to intersex numbers and related data from research provided by the professional staff at the Lurie Children's Hospital and Mr. Eric Villian at UCLA.

56 At present, LGTBQ stands for Lesbian, Gay, Transgender, Bisexual, and Queer (some regions of America refer to *Q* as "questioning").

57 John 8: 3–11.

Chapter 9

58 *Funk and Wagnalls Standard Dictionary.* s.v. "ceremony."

59 Ibid., s.v. "ritual."

60 Ibid., s.v. "rite."

61 Ibid., s.v. "symbol."

62 Ibid., s.v. "sign."

63 McKenzie, *Dictionary of the Bible,* 251.

64 *Encyclopedia Britannica: Micropedia,* s.v. "Franciscan."

65 McKenzie, *Dictionary of the Bible,* 642–543.

66 *Encyclopedia Britannica: Macropedia,* s.v. "the sacraments."

67 Matthew 18:20.

68 Rahner and Vorgrimler, *Dictionary of Theology,* 291–292; 347–348.

69 Ibid.

70 Mark 6:5.

71 *Encyclopedia Britannica: Macropedia,* s.v. "sacrament."

72 Ephesians 5:25.

73 Statistics provided by Adelaide Mena, *Catholic News Agency*, October 1, 2013; also Michael Paulson, *New York Times*, January 24, 2015.

74 The reader may wish to look into the reason for a major schism during the reign of Henry VIII (sixteenth century CE). The institution of the Church of England, and consequent invasion into Europe, resulted in serious damage to the Roman Catholic Church. Although no one could say Rome's insistence on control of marriage matters led to all the problems at that time, it is my belief that the birth of a major schism in the Church had its source in someone living "in sin" with another woman.

Chapter 10

75 https:wwwcatholicculture.org/culture/librarydictionary/index. cfmpid=36571.

76 Genesis 22:17.

77 Matthew 22:23–33. Reference is to Jesus's argument with the Sadducees regarding marriage in the afterlife.

78 Gerry Leisman, Ahmed Moustafa, and Tal Shafir, "Thinking, Waking, Talking: Integretory Motor and Cognitive Brain Function," *Frontiers in Public Health*, May 26, 2016.

79 Allan Snyder, "Does the Brain Possess Potential Super Powers?" *Daily Galaxy*, March 25, 2008, Sidney, Australia. A mind expert, Allan Snyder of the University of Sidney, director of Centre for the Mind, writes the article. This relates to studies done on autistic savants that carry superpowers. They exhibit brain functions that can store what scientists believe could be an infinite amount of knowledge.

Chapter 11

80 Horace's Ode 3.30.6 *The Ode on Immortality*.

81   Teilhard de Chardin, *The Divine Milieu* (New York: Harper Torchbook, 1968), 140–143.

82   The Lemaitre-Eddington model looked at the universe expanding as from a "primeval atom" or "cosmic egg," which was understood not as an explosion, but a subparticle nuclear event.

83   Recommended for additional information: "What's in a Name: History and Meanings of the Term Big Bang," by Helge Kragh; published through the Centre for Science Studies, Department of Physics and Astronomy, Aarhus University, Aarhus, Denmark. This resource was obtained from a major work by this author.

84   Stephen Hawking, *A Brief History of Time: From the Big Bang to Black Holes*, (Toronto: Bantam Books, 1988).

85   Stephen Hawking, ed. *A Brief History of Time: A Reader's Companion* (New York: Bantam Books, 1992), 185. Further refining of what the big bang means is explained by singularity, which occurred at the beginning the universe when all the universe was at a single point of infinite density and temperature. Such an event is outside the scope of science at this time.

86   *The New Lexicon Webster's Encyclopedic Dictionary*, s.v. "archetype." The word is defined as the model from which later examples are developed.

87   1 Corinthians 15:17.

Chapter 12

88   There is no accepted proof for the existence of God. All supposed intellectual arguments are widely criticized. Most theists rely on their prior beliefs for support. The consensus today is that some act of faith will have to bridge this gap of not having a reasonable and convincing proof that God exists.

89 Wikipedia, s.v. "Yuri Gargarin." https://en.wikipedia.org/wiki/ Yuri-Gargarin.

90 Richard Dawkins, taken from "Richard Dawkins Quotes," *Brainy Quote* website. https://www.brainyquote.com/authors/richard_dawkins.

Bibliography

Abraham, Carolyn, Sarah Barmak, Colby Cosh, Rosemary Counter, Gaeta Dayal, Katherine DeClerq, Jonathon Gatehouse, Charlie Gillis, David Graham, Hanna Hoag, Matt Kwong, Nick Taylor-Faisey, Emma Teitel, and Rosemary Westwood. *The New Brain: Maclean's Special Edition.* Toronto: Rogers Publishing Limited, 2013.

Applewhite, E. J. *Paradise Mislaid.* New York: St. Martin's Press, 1991.

Ayala, Francisco J. *Darwin's Gift to Science and Religion.* Washington, DC: Joseph Henry Press, 2007.

Buckingham, Will, Douglas Burnham, Clive Hill, Peter J. King, John Marenbon, and Marcus Weeks. *The Philosophy Book: Big Ideas Simply Explained.* New York: DK Publishing, 2011.

Copleston, Frederick, SJ. *A History of Philosophy. Vol. 1, Greece and Rome: From the Pre-Socratics to Plotinus.* New York: Doubleday, 1993.

Copleston, Frederick, SJ. *A History of Philosophy. Vol. 2, Mediaeval Philosophy. New York* :Doubleday, 1962.

The Dalai Lama. *The Universe in a Single Atom.* New York: Morgan Road Books, 2005.

de Chardin, Pierre Teilhard, SJ. *The Divine Milieu.* New York: Harper TorchBooks, 1968.

de Chardin, Pierre Teilhard, SJ. *Man's Place in Nature.* New York: Harper and Row, 1966.

de Chardin, Pierre Teilhard, SJ. *The Phenomenon of Man.* New York: Harper TorchBooks, 1965.

Dunbar, Robin. *Human Evolution: Our Brains and Behavior.* London: Oxford University Press, 2016.

Ehrman, Bart D. *Misquoting Jesus.* San Francisco: Harper, 2005.

Encyclical Letter of Pope Paul VI: On the Regulation of Birth. Boston: Daughters of St. Paul, 1968.

Encyclopedia Britannica. Chicago: William Benton, Publisher, 1974.

Fremantle, Anne, ed. *The Papal Encyclicals in Their Historical Context.* New York: The New American Library, 1956.

Funk and Wagnalls Standard Dictionary. New York: Funk and Wagnalls, 1974.

Hawking, Stephen W. *A Brief History of Time: From the Big Bang to Black Holes.* Toronto: Bantam Books, 1988.

Hawking, Stephen W., ed. *A Brief History of Time: A Reader's Companion.* New York: Bantam Books, 1992.

Henig, Robin Marantz. "Rethinking Gender." *National Geographic*, January 2017. 48–73.

Hughes, Philip. *The Church in Crisis: A History of the General Councils 325–1870*. New York: Hanover House, 1961.

Isaacson, Walter. *Einstein*. New York: Simon and Schuster, 2007.

The Jerusalem Bible: Reader's Edition. New York: Doubleday, 1968.

Kalb, Claudia. "Genius." *National Geographic*, May 2017. 30–33.

Martel, Yann. *The High Mountains of Portugal*. Toronto: Alfred A. Knopf, 2016.

McKenzie, John L., SJ. *Dictionary of the Bible*. Milwaukee: Bruce Publishing Company, 1965.

A New Catechism: Catholic Faith for Adults. New York: Herder and Herder, 1971.

Rahner, Karl, and Herbert Vorgrimler. *Theological Dictionary*. New York: Herder and Herder, 1968.

Shreeve, Jamie. "Mystery Man." *National Geographic*, October 2015. 30–56.

Strong, James, STD, LLD. *The Exhaustive Concordance of the Bible*. Massachusetts: Hendrickson Publishers.

Talpalariu, Dan. "Pope Benedict Meets Stephen Hawking: The Pontiff Agrees to Empirical Science as an Act of God." *Softpedia News*, November 3, 2008. http://www.news.softpedia.com/new/Pope-Benedict-Meets-Stephen-Hawking.

Webster's Encyclopedic Dictionary: Canada Edition. New York: Lexicon Publications, 1988.

Zanzig, Thomas. *Jesus of History: Christ of Faith.* Minnesota: St Mary's Press, 1982.

CPSIA information can be obtained
at www.ICGtesting.com
Printed in the USA
LVHW03s2108100918
589689LV00002B/342/P